LADAKH BUDDHIST CULTURE AND TRADITION

LADAKH BUDDHIST CULTURE AND TRADITION

PREM SINGH JINA

PUBLICATIONS

KALPAZ PUBLICATIONS

DELHI-110052

Ladakh Buddhist Culture and Tradition

Rs. 690

ISBN: 81-7835-564-7

Published in 2007 in India by
Kalpaz Publications
C-30, Satyawati Nagar,
Delhi-110052
E-mail: kalpaz@hotmail.com
Phone : 9212729499

Lasser Type Setting by: Rudra Computer Graphics, Delhi
Printed at : Salasar Imaging System, Delhi

Dedicated To

Mrs. Manju Jina

Contents

Preface

Ladakh is a wonderful land lies in the lap of Trans Himalayas. In olden days it was popular for trade to Central Asia. In 1947, when India got Independence, Ladakh became an integral part of Indian Republic. Pakistan did not want this, attacked Ladakh four times viz. 1948, 1965, 1971, and 1999. Its north and western borders touch China. In 1962 after taking opportunity China also invaded Ladakh and captured a large area. Thereafter, it became an important issue for Indian Government to take care of this remote border land and to develop it under the direction of defence personals. Today development plans are undertaken by Autonomous Hill Development Councils – Leh and Kargil in a democratic way.

This book covers eighteen chapters based on my research work and observations in Ladakh. In brief it is divided in three parts:

(i) General study : Role of kings, trade transport, society and hygiene.

(ii) Festival : Losar.

(iii) History and Culture : A study of Buddhist monasteries, Tibetan manuscripts and inscriptions.

I hope the outcome of this work though general but interesting for students, teachers and tourists.

The author may accept some shortcoming in this academic presentation as he is working under terrible constraints of hostile climatic conditions, linguistic communication problems and unfavourable administrative support.

Dr. Prem Singh Jina

Acknowledgements

I would like to express my deep appreciation and gratitude to Prof. Maya Ram (Retd.), Director U.P. Higher Education, Allahabad, who inspired me in the field of Ladakh studies.

I wish to take this opportunity to express my deep appreciation and heartful thanks to Dr. (Mrs.) Kapila Vatsayan (Retd.), Secretary, Department of Culture, Ministry of Tourism and Culture, New Delhi.

I am also grateful to the authors, and my Lamas students, by whose thought and works I have been benefited immensely.

I express thanks to Kalpaz Publications Delhi and Mrs Manju Jina, Principal, Hira Convent School, Bari Mukhani, Haldwani who always encouraged me to write on Ladakh.

Dr. Prem Singh Jina

List of Figures

List of Figures

List of Tables

List of Appendices

Abbreviation

POK : Pakistan Occupied Kashmir.
SNM : Sonam Norbu Memorial.

List of Illustrations

Introduction

The historical picture of Ladakh before the First Dynasty is not clear. Though the sketchy inscriptions found near Kha-la-tse we can understand that once it was under Kushana empire. However, Chinese pilgrims, came to India via Trans Himalaya, did not say anything about Ladakh. In lower Ladakh Dardi-speaking people had some cultivated lands, but maximum of them had nomadic life. They may be influenced by Buddhism, as Kashmir in those days was one of the principal Buddhist center in India. The Sarada inscriptions at Dras and Chingtan are the evidences in this regards. The Sogdian inscriptions found on boulders at Tangtse (Tib. grang tse), indicate that before 10th century many Sogdian Christian and Arabian merchants visited upto the higher reaches of Ladakh for trade, but I don't know why did they not penetrate upper or lower Ladakh? In fact till 9-10th century there was no ruler in Ladakh. After the fall of the Tibetan monarchy Ladakh Kingdom came into light. Palgyigon founded the Ladakh kingdom, he was the first king of Ladakh dynasty. This dynasty was mostly ruled by Tibetans except Utpala, who is supposed to be of Aryan stream. Till 15th Century we don't know much the role of Ladakhi kings. During 15th Century Geluk-pa school spread in Ladakh with the kind support of Dragspa Bumde. Earlier to him Lotsava Rinchen Zangpo made an inspiring efforts to build temples in Ladakh. Popular among them are Alchi, Nar-ma and Sumda monasteries.

The Second Dynasty of Ladakh was tentatively founded by Lhachen Bhagan. King Bhagan had two sons, he gave them Namgyal title. Thereafter kings given name 'Namgyal', hence called Namgyal Dynasty. It has a list of fourteen kings in sequence (1460-1842). Tashi Namgyal erected a castle on the summit on a hillock near Leh called Namgyal Tsemo. According to Ladakh chronicles king Tashi Namgyal fought bravely against the invading force of Hor and killed many. Later he erected the above castle and just below Gonkhang temple on the corpses of the slain Mongols. King Tashi was by nature a religious person. He had faith on all the Buddhist orders of Mahayana, and invited Chos je Dan ma to build a monastery in his kingdom. Jamyang Namgyal's regime may be considered as period of darkness. Shia Muslim population in his kingdom migrated from Baltistan in large number and settled down along Indus banks near Leh and Phyang village. Singge Namgyal was the greatest king of Ladakh during 17th century. He had warlike ability and was able to extend the boundary of his kingdom. In his regime Drugpa a suborder of the K'agyud pa became very influential position in Ladakh. Hemis of this order was established during 17th century.

King Deldan Namgyal thereafter built a long mani wall near Leh and erected three stories high Buddha statue in Sheh. During his regime Mughals put military pressure to accept Islam, consequently a mosque was built at Leh.

Tsepal Namgyal was the last king in the Second Dynasty of Ladakh. In his regime Zorawar Singh invaded Ladakh and put it under the domination of Maharaja Gulab Singh. In 1947 India got independence, Jammu & Kashmir state became a part of India, Ladakh too also came under Indian Republic. Pakistan did not digest this incident, captured Skardu and some portion of Zoji-la pass; some Pakistani troops even reached near Leh up to Taru village. But Indian troops arrived at Leh and Kashmir, after ferocious tanks battle at Zoji-La, Indian army recaptured Zoji-la, then Kargil. Some Indian troops dropped directly by air at Leh.Pakistani forces had their tents at Nimo and its adjoining areas. Indian troops attacked them both sides from Leh as well from Basgo. They were unable to defend Indian forces and ran away to Skardo. Finally cease fire took place. Pakistan thence illegally occupied Skardo and other neighbouring areas called POK.

Ladakh had witnessed four wars – The first with China in 1962, later in 1965, 1971 and 1999 with Pakistan. The 1962 war against China had opened Indian Government eyes. China in this war occupied a large Indian territory including Akasi Chin. Thereafter Indian government focused its attention for infrastructure development. In 1974 Ladakh was opened for foreigners, as a result it came in the world tourist map. During Atal Behari Vajpayee Government period Sindhu Darshan Festival widely advertised in India. Many domestic pilgrim tourists visited Ladakh. Today Ladakh annually receives more than 35,000 tourists. Indian tourist population has been increasing year after year. The living standard of Ladakhis has been increased considerably, more and more hotels, guest houses, restaurants etc. are taking place at Leh and Kargil areas. Therefore, Ladakh Autonomous Hill Councils of Leh and Kargil will have to watch such activities carefully so that the Ladakh environment and landscape may not be disturbed.

1

King Deldan Namgyal (Tib. bde – ldan rnam rgyal)

Deldan Namgyal was the eldest son of Singge Namgyal[1], later became the king of Ladakh, however, his younger brothers – Indra Bodhi[2] and Dechog Namgyal[3] became Vassal kings; after some time king made several plans and also decided to restore the lost prestige. He sent his army under the command of his minister, Lonpo Zorwa Gyatso[4], as Field-Marshal to attack Purig[5]. In 1638 under the command of Agu[6] Karmo Ladakhi force entered in Purig[7], reconquered his lost province.[8]

Marched to Baltistan

In 1639, Ladakh Army marched for Baltistan, attacked Kapalu. Hu Sen Khan was the Duke of Kapalu, he fought bravely, but defeated. Thereafter, Ladakh Army conquered Chorbar and Tortskar villages; when Ladakhi soldiers were about to enter Skardo, Balti queen Khathun immediately asked military help from Kashmir Nawab, subsequently with his intervention 20,000 Turk soldiers marched for Ladakh. However, as they reached at Pasari, Ladakh Army under the command of Kalon Drug Namgyal stopped Turks, ferocious fighting took place, Ladakhis fought bravely, killed many Turks, their flags and kettle-drums were taken by them and, gained victory over the enemy. In the meanwhile Temur Beg with Skardu Army reached

Bodhkharbu, battle against Ladakh Army took place. Finally war was ended with agreement.[9]

Visit of Jesuit Andrada

In 1624 Father Antoniod' Andrala, sent from Goa, surmounted the dangers and hardship of a journey through the Lower Himalayan zone succeeded to enter in Ladakh. He met king Deldan Namgyal. In Ladakh he was given warm welcome by king and his cabinet, on his request, king gave him some D.O. letters at the name of Tibetan authorities so that he could be allowed in Guge. Thus Andrada via Ladakh entered in Tasaparang, capital of the West Tibetan kingdom of Guge'. There he founded Christian missionary center.

Popular song against Baltis

Ladakh Army several times defeated Baltis, as a result they were being praised by Balties as mentioned in the following folk song :

"............Thou turnest back the Turk army of Skardo on the Daltong Pass.........

Lighting fleshes out of king Deldan Namgyal's sword."[10]

Religious Works

He built one of the longest mani-wall near Leh about 850 paces (or about 2050 feet) and Namgyal chortens both of its ends. It was built in the memory of his mother, later erected at Sheh a Buddha image of clay, copper and gilt, three stories in height (or about 40 feet) for the spiritual welfare of his father. This image has precious things and about 7.50 kg gold inside its main stand. This image was erected during 1641 with the help of Nepali and Ladakhi artists named : Agu Karmo, Saktipa Saki Tonspon Seldok, Palbo Sangyas, Zingpa Namgyal, Paldan Tsering Gyatso, Dewa Tsering, etc.[11]

There is also a 71 feet high chorten near to the above temple in which Buddha image is placed.[12] On this chorten the following inscription is written :

Text in Classical Language

aō bkra shis

bla ma stag gi phyag can yin

rgyal po sgeng ge phyag can yin
rgyal mo ka b'ai phyag can yin
chos blo 'agu dkar mo yin

Roman Transliteration

Om Tashis
Lama stag gi chag can yin
Gyalpo Singge chag can yin
Gyalmo Kave chag can yin
Chos lo Agu Karmo yin

Translation

Om Tashis (sarvamangalam !) (I pray) to Lama Stagtsang (Salute to) King Singge namgyal (of Ladakh) (I pay my regards to) queen (of Ladakh) (Salute to) Lonpo Agu Karmo (all who erected the Buddha image).

Besides King Deldan Namgyal built another Buddha and Avalokitesvara images of about 20 feet high at the Leh palace and one silver chorten. All these are placed in Assembly Hall (or Du-khang).[13] of Leh palace.

Notes & References

1. Singge Namgyal : He was the king of Ladakh and son of Jamyang Namgyal from his second wife Gyal Khatun.
2. Indra Bodhi (Tib. ai nbra bo dhi) : He was the principal disciple of Stag-tsang raspa, the great guru of Drugpa Kargyud order of Buddhism, later became the ruler of Guge province.
3. Dechog Namgyal (Tib. bde mchog rnam rgyal) : He was the youngest son of Singge Namgyal, became vassal king of Zangskar and Spiti. Cf. Francke, A.H. : 'A history of Western Tibet',Reprinted by Asian Educational Services, New Delhi; 1995:101.
4. Lonpo Zorwa Gyatso (Tib. blon po 'abyor ba rgya mtsho) : He was a brave soldier of Ladakh Army.
5. Purig : It consisted the area between Zoji-la and Fotu-la. Its principal villages are Mulbek, Pashkyum, Kargil and Dras.

Besides Kartse, Darkit, Lotsum, Pashkyum, Skambu, Tatsa-Karit, Yubaltak, Tumet etc. are Muslim dominant villages.

6. Agu Karmo : Tib. agu 'gar mo. He had leadership quality and was able to lead his army.
7. While entering in Purig Ladakh Army at first invaded the Tri Sultan territory, he was the Duke of Kartse and had independent kingdom from Karbu to Dras. Thereafter, invaded the another Duke of Purig called Sultan of Chigtan and taken Chigtan and Shagkar castles. Finally Ladakh Army before returning to Leh attacked the three castles: Stod (a little north of Kargil), Sumtang and Kartse of Tri Sultan. The Field Marshal of Ladakh Army taken Tri Sultan to Leh as prisoner. Cf. Francke, A.H.: 'A History of Western Tibet', *op. cit.*;102-03.
8. Francke, A.H.; *op. cit.* :103 and Phungtsog: 'Ladakh' : 135.
9. Francke, A.H.; *op. cit.* : 103.
10. Francke, A.H.; op. cit. : 104. Here follows the two popular songs collected by him : "At the Lake Mondur, stobsyabgoba appears and shows his strategy. The god-like force of Skardo cast their lhassos of steel. They pay back to the god-like army of Ladakh what is their due. They revenge their fathers and forefathers on them. The children of the lord of Shigar gain a glorious victory." "The lord resides at the flower-castle of Saling. God is gracious to thee. This summer ! The king resides at the flower- castle of Saling. God is giving success to thee this summer ! Thou turnest back the Turk army of Skardo on the Daltong Pass.God is gracious to thee this summer! Thou dictatest a treaty to them, to last longer than a lifetime. Lightning flashes out of King Deldan Namgyal's sword."
11. Francke, A.H. ; *op.cit.* : 103 and Phungtsog; *op. cit.* :135.
12. *Ibid.*
13. Francke, A.H. ; *op. cit.* : 103.

2

Fall of Ladakh Kingdom

Tsepal dondrub namgyal (or Tsepal Namgyal) became king of Ladakh after the death of his brother Tsestan Namgyal, who died by smallpox which broke in Leh during (1800-1810).[1] Tesepal Namgyal was a lama at Hemis monastery. He was requested to take the throne of Ladakh as Tsestan Namgyal died childless in young age (i.e. 24 years of age). Later Tsepal Namgyal turned layman. He inherited from his brother not only the kingdom but also his wife Spal Chung, from whom he got one son.[2]

Tsepal loved easy life. He had no faith on his ministers. When he came on thorne, had changed all ministers of his brother's time and ordered:

"All high ranked officers and ministers in his kingdom will not be allowed to sleep at night and will have to stick vigilant with his assigned work and kingdom."[3]

He ordered to supply 12 *chabskyang* full water only during night instead at morning to the officers and ministers. Besides he himself took surprise visits during night hours.[4] Francke remarks :

"He seems to inherited the taint of madness from his father; for many strange things are told about him. The private servants in the palace had to promise daily not to sleep at night. The king also did not sleep at night. He rose when the sun grew hot. In the morning, when washing his hands, he required twelve or thirteen basin full of cold and hot water. When he traveled about in the provinces he went at night, and then with lamps and torches"[5]

Without any strong reason, he after the discussion with Giva Gonpo ordered to put king of Zanskar and the Purig Kalon (minister) in prison.[6]

Moorcroft during his regime wanted to meet him. But on the advice of Kalon Tsewang Tondup, Nono Kalon, Leh Lonpo Tsenzin Namgyal and mother Gyalmo he did not allow. However, with the presence of Mir Izzadulla on 21st October 1820 king agreed. In presence of Kalon Tsewang Tondup, Nono Kalon, Kaga Tsenzin, Mosim Baba Horpa, Abdul Latif and some employees to palace king meet with the team of Moorcroft. They presented a variety of things including guns and said :

"We have come to see the way in which your ministers and people behave, and your majesty's wisdom; and as there is a likelihood of this country being conquered, if we built a tower (fort) here it would prove useful to the king."[7]

The king and his ministers after considering the case, said : "If they would build a fort, no one knows what means of doing harm it may be! And did not allow them to build it in the following grounds that :

1. We may loose administrative power, a time may come they will rule on us.
2. If we allow them, it will hinder our good relations with the businessmen who have their shops at Leh market and those who come here from Central Asian countries for trade.
3. They may impose taxes.
4. Via Niti la if trade will open with Tibet throughout the year they will have more benefit than us."[8]

Moorcroft team men after staying two summers and one winter in Leh droped a letter in box and said:

"Accept this; it may cure the king's mind!"[9]

Moorcropt with his team returned to Kashmir on 20th September 1822.[10]

At the time of Nyiungti Kalon and Kharpon Kaga Rabgis, Kulu invaders entered Spiti, after destroying villagers' property, carried away yak, horses, sheep, goats and other important things. Spiti was then under Ladakh kingdom, when villagers petitioned Tsepal that he should wage a war of revenge, but without any sympathy king said: "You have not tried your best!" and punished them.[11]

Thereafter viewing the weakness of Tsepal Namgyal Kulu invaders again decided to invade Ladakh. This time they included Lahul army and invaded Zanskar. Destroyed monasteries, taken away precious statues, from villages stole ponies, yaks and whatever there was important, then returned without any interruption. Invaders activities were not stopped here, an army general of Paldar Ratan Sher Khan with his small group of soldiers invaded Zanskar, destroyed all the villages between Ating and Padum. Anyhow peace took place. The king Tsepal Namgyal again did not make any efforts for the safeguard of Zanskar region.[12]

After one year Kishtawar army invaded upper Zanskar region and reached inside Zanskar upto Dung-ring. Invaders destroyed and burnt the villages with fire, carried away wealth and cattle. Thus, Lower Ladakh, particularly Zanskar region became the prey to neighbouring invaders. In the mean while Tsepal Namgyal's laziness behaviour reached to Jammu.[13]

On the other hand king Tsepal Namgyal decided to build palace at Stok village, opposite to Leh. Besides with the help of Kalon Tsewang Tondup he erected many idols, here follows some of them:[14]

1. Vajrapani (Tib. Phyagna-rdo–rje) with gold head.
2. Silver chorten : Height one storey.
3. Guru Padmasambhava (or Guru Padma od mar), made of silver.
4. Vajrapani, made of silver for Thakchen Kongma, Leh.
5. Tsepagmed, made of silver for Sheh.
6. White Tara.

This was the time when Kalon Tsewang Tondup at the age of 54 years died.[15] Thereafter other Kalons and Lopons came to know king's laziness and started to befooling him. They said :

"Possibly Skardo Cho will attack Ladakh, we should send our army there so that Cho's army would not enter in Ladakh."[16]

King agreed and sent Ladakh army under the command of two Kalons to Skardo. After some time they returned to Leh and said:

"His Majesty! We did well in war."[17]

King became happy and presented one box tea to each and distributed cloths, salt, wood etc. among soldiers.[18]

He put Mulbek Kalon and his family in Chushod jail without any reason, however 'Cho' and his Chagzot Namgyal was released. By the time his eldest son Tsewang Rabstan Namgyal died; for the interest of his kingdom he had to please his second son Chogsprul Namgyal, who was a child and had different nature, Lama Yangdzin ngapa then discovered that prince was the incarnation of the great Lama Bhilva Dorji. Prince was obedient of his mother, on her advice he started to take part in parties, young girls were invited for his amusement who offered chhang (wine) and dance. Finally he married the younger daughter of the minister Tsewang Dondrubi, Skalzang Dolma. Having once tasted the sweetness of matrimony, he married yet Tsunmo Palskyid, of Pashkyum and Zora Khatun. It was the time when Dogra army arrived upto Kartse.[19]

In 1828 war between Gyanak (China) and Yarkand took place. Yarkand King Abdul Sattar with the help of other Hor soldiers defended his country for about two years, later he along with 1000 soldiers and 700 horse riders left the battle field, unfortunately forgotten the route. It was winter season, many horses and soldiers were died due to snow storm. 300 soldiers and 250 horse riders left behind. They reached near Shyok. Later with the help of 'ca-sa-tak-Ju', 'ku-cak-sol-dok' and 'Tangtse Kharpon' arrived Leh after 11 days journey. Some of them stayed *Umla's* residence and others stayed at *Hemi Latang'*.[20] After some time they met king Tsepal Namgyal, offered valuable things and horses to king and said :

"For the sake of god we reached here, now would like to go for Haj."[21]

King Tsepal conducted a meeting of his ministers. One minister Kaga Tsenzing of Hundar, Nubra said :

"China is a Buddhist country, Yarkandis and others who were involved in China war are enemy of Buddhists, therefore, we should return prisoners of war to China."[22]

King without discussing further written a letter to China to take their enemies. After two and half month China king sent 40 soldiers and 50 horse rides with hand cuffs. Yarkand king sattar and his men were taken into custody and sent to them to China. To

know Ladakh king's such unfavourable decision, Abdul Sattar became very sad and cursed ladakh King:[23]

"May god, Ladakh king and his son die boil pain and his kingdom may be taken by others"[24]

On the 16th of August 1834, Zorawar Singh with his 10,000 men reached Kartse. Ladakhi force of about 5000, marched under the command of the young minister of stok. At Sanku they tried to stop the movement of stormy Dogra force, but unable to do so. Dogras captured Pashkyum and Sod regions. When winter was over Dogra force again moved further. At Mulbek Ladakhi army again tried to stop them, mild resentment by Ladakh army couldn't do anything. At last Dogra force reached at Basgo, here first time Zorawar Singh had a meeting with king Tsepal Namgyal, who in fact came for peace negotiation. Zorawar Singh later went to Leh with a small number of soldiers as guard while moving to Leh he secretly ordered his juniors, after sometime you would also move behind us. The second part of the agreement took place at Leh under which King Tsepal was asked to pay an annual tribute of 20,000 rupees. Besides, he was order to pay 50,000 rupees on spot towards the war expenses. At the end King Tsepal Namgyal deposed in 1837, reinstalled in 1839, finally according to King Abdul Sattar's sad voice he had been suffered by boil pain, and in 1840 he died. Thereafter ladakh was included under Maharaja of Jammu and Kashmir Reyashad, When J & K state became a part of India in 1947, Ladakh too came under Indian Republic[25].

Notes & References

1. Gergen, Joseph: 'bla-dvags-rgyal-rabs' ci-med gter' New Delhi, 1976: 493 & Francke, A History of Western Tibet', Asian Educational Services, New Delhi, 1995 (Reprinted): 128.
2. *Ibid.*
3. Gergen, Joseph; *op.cit.*: 493.
4. *Ibid.*
5. Francke, A.H.; op.cit.:128.
6. *Ibid.*, 129.
7. *Ibid.,* 129-130.
8. Gergen, Joseph; *op.cit.* : 496 & Francke, A.H.; *op.cit*:130.

9. Francke, A.H.; *op.cit.*:130.
10. Gergen, Joseph; *op.cit.*: 497.
11. Francke, A.H.; *op.cit.*:130-31.
12. Gergen, Joseph; *op.cit.*:498 and Francke, A.H.; *op.cit.*:131.
13. *Ibid.*
14. Gergen, Joseph; *op.cit.* ; 498-99 and Francke A.H.; *op.cit*: 132.
15. Gergen, Joseph; *op.cit.*:498.
16. *Ibid.*:499.
17. *Ibid.*
18. *Ibid.*
19. Gergen, Joseph; *op.cit.*: 499 and Francke, A.H.; *op.cit*: 133.
20. Gergen, Joseph; *op. cit*: 499.
21. *Ibid.*
22. *Ibid.*
23. *Ibid.*
24. *Ibid.*
25. Francke, A. H.; *op.cit.*:145-147.

Dorje chenmo

Ruins of Nyarma monastery

Padmasambhava in
New Dorje chenmo temple,
Nyarma monastery

Sakyamumi Buddha with his
principal disciples in
New Dorje chenmo
temple, Nyarma

16 Arhats in New Dolje chenmo temple Nyarma monastery

Maitreya in Coktsal Gonpa

Avalokitesvara statne in
Coktsal Gonpa

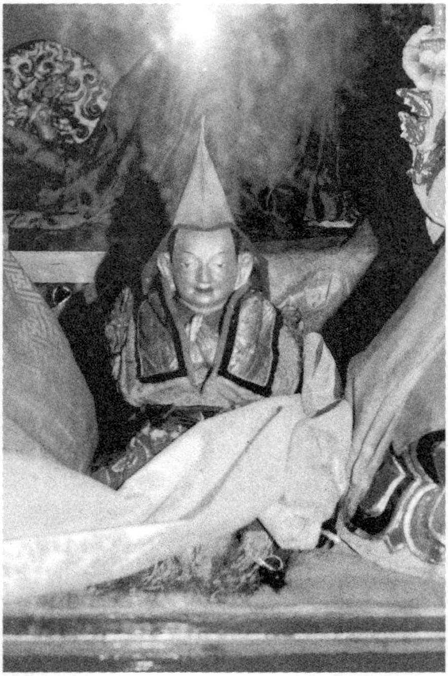

Trongkhapa Statne in
Coktsal Gonpa

3

Res System in Ladakh during 1900-1920

Res system is defined as by which a village or group of villages has to supply transport[1] at a certain stage on a certain time.

In olden days Central Asian traders[2] were needed transport at each allotted stage. The system had some drawbacks as stated below :[3]

(i) Ladakhi villages had limited resources, they had limited number of livestock available for transport during summer season.

(ii) To fulfill the increasing transport animals demand by traders villagers had to use their only a few animals, as a result annually large number of ponies died for want of fodder.

(iii) Villagers some time had to sale their ponies into the hands of traders. This tradition caused less number of ponies at the allotted stages.

(iv) When traders didn't get ponies as required, they had to stay for some days, persistent complaints in this regards reached to the higher authorities. Accordingly, the higher authority directed to local authorities to supply necessary transport, thus villagers were bound to overloaded their animals. Consequently became unfit for further service.

(v) Begars were unevenly distributed among the different villages. Again some groups of villages were required to remain at the stages in their entire strength, which seriously interfered with their agricultural operations. Because Buddhist didn't have good number of human labours as they used to adopt polyandry system. The excess human population either became lamas or chomos at their respective gonpas. Thus left behind less nember of people who had to operate in their agriculture field under co-operative system. Therefore, during cultivation season villages in Ladakh did not have people to work as Begars or go with transport.

(vi) Large exemptions had been given in each village by competent and incompetent authorities, viz. Tahsildars , Kardars, village officers etc. were exempted. These exemptions hampered the Res arrangements by reducing the number of men liable to Kar-begar.

Under the Res system at each stage villagers of Ladakh had to arrange average 36 ponies, and 21 coolies during summers and average 23 coolies during winters. The Tahsildar of the concerned areas having the power to reduce the requirements of ponies or coolies. The following persons were entitled to use Res transport :

1. Public servants.
2. Bonafide travelers whether Europeans or others.
3. Central Asian traders.

The above would carry their personal baggage and merchandise in case of traders.

While providing Res facilities to the concerned the following points had to be noted by the local authorities under the direction of higher authority.

1. Public servants have the first claim to Res, after them travelers, and lastly traders within each of the three classes of persons mentioned; individuals may claim Res in order of their arrival at the stage.
2. Res transport is not allowed to Public Works Department for carrying timber and other materials, from place to place.
3. The term 'Public servant' includes Public Works Department contractors for their personal baggage but not for stores and materials.
4. Maximum weight of a pony or cooly load is fixed as follows :
   (i) Pony load 2.5 maunds.

(ii) Cooly load summer 35 and winter 25 seers that is to say three coolies per pony load in summer and 4 in winter.

5. No transport to be used without full payment, carrying wages on the treaty high road are fixed by the British Joint Commissioner and on other roads by the Wazir Wazarat. No person shall used the Res transport without the wages so fixed.
6. Res transport to be kept on the road. Special arrangements for requirements off the road. The Res transport of Dras and Kharbu shall be used on Leh road and on the Shardu road as far as Khanal. For all purposes off the road arrangements at the above name stages will have to be made through the Zaildar of Dras independently of the Res.
7. For trips off the road – For other cases than those mentioned above Res transport shall not be used for more than one stage nor detained for more than one day.
8. Limit for the use of lies transport – Res transport shall not be used beyond the next stage on the road on other sides of the starting point, with the exception that the Res at Dras is used up to Gund in the direction of Kashmir.
9. Use of Res transport by the state officials not entitled to traveling allowance – state officials not entitled to traveling allowance when traveling on duty on the main road. Roads may use Res transport without payment for personal baggage and state things usually carried with them. They shall not use riding ponies without paying for them unless specially authorized to do so by the Wazir Wazarat or Tahsildar under a written order.
10. A limit of one cooly is fixed for Patwaris and menials and that of two for officials of superior grade for their personal luggage. The carriage of personal luggage of the Wazarat Chaprasis entitled to traveling allowance will be paid from contingencies.
11. Limit use of transport supplied under Rule 9. The transport mentioned in the proceeding rule will be used more than that carriage on the road.
12. Res Register has to be completed.

13. No person shall demand transport during the period required by the said transport to return from its destination.
14. If cannot wait make special arrangements at voluntary rates. Those who cannot wait till return of the said transport will have to make their own arrangements from the surrounding villages at voluntary rates.
15. Full groups of villages responsible for requirements of camps staying outside regular stages. In case of a large camp staying in a village where there is no regular stage its requirements of transport shall be met in due proportion by the group of villages to which that village belongs under the Res arrangements.
16. Respas not be used for personal service. No officials shall use Res coolies, locally called Respas, for his personal service at the headquarters of Tehsils or when in camp."

Rules in relation to supply ration under Res system[4]

1. State Kothis were responsible to supply grain from the following :

(a)	Dras	On the Leh road
(b)	Kargil	
(c)	Lamayuru	
(d)	Saspol	
(e)	Leh	
(f)	Panamic	
(g)	Kharal	On the Skardu
(h)	Olding	
(i)	Tarkati	
(j)	Kharmang	
(k)	Parkuta	
(l)	Skardu	
(m)	Thor	

The State Kothis used to keep the following items:[5]

1. Wheat and grim.
2. Wheat and grim might be kept as whole or in Atta.
3. If required concerned authority arranged demanded items from the shopkeepers at Dras, Kargil, Leh and Skardu at market rates.

4. Visitors, traders and officials who were traveling on duty, entitled to get grain from the Kothis according to their entitlement.

Supply of Firewood, Grass and Other Items[6]

State Kothis didn't supply firewood or grass. Officials got the same from Res free of charge under the condition that the concerned should be on duty. For other supplies such as butter, milk, fowls, eggs, sheep, oil, etc. Contractors had been appointed by the British Joint Commissioner at every state on the road.

At the end I would say under the Res system travelers and traders were given all necessary facilities at each stage on the Srinagar to Leh as well as Srinagar to Skardu via Kargil road. Leh and Skardu were then Central Asian trade *mundies*. The trade activities were jointly controlled by British Government Joint Commissioner and Wazir Wazarat Jammu & Kashmir Riyashad. The Res system was also look after by them jointly.

Notes and References

1. Transport means that includes men and animals used for carrying passengers and animals from place to place.
2. Central Asian traders : Those who enter trade directly with Central Asia who come to Leh in order to trade with those trading with Central Asia.
3. Prelimary report of Ladakh settlement by Chaudhri Khushi Mohamad; 1908:25.
4. Kargil Res Rules: 17th June 1912 sanction of his Highness the Maharaja R. Sahib Bahadur to Res Rules for the whole district of Ladakh.
5. *Ibid.*
6. *Ibid.*

4

Buddhist Traditional Society and Economic Development in Ladakh

Traditional society can be explained by the habits, customs, attitudes, and ways of life and means of the concerned people of the society. It also means that a society which has a certain rigidity in order to preserve its identity. However, adjustment of some changes according to the voice of young generation may stimulate. The traditional system, can also mean values independent of time, including values that are essentially dated in character. A traditional society doesn't mean a backward society, but it can be progressive in some of its content.

In Ladakh Buddhist society and its economy during king regime (Fig. 4.1). based upon polyandry system. As a result one female shared sexual relations with two or more brothers in the family. Thus caused low population growth and excess male and female were donated to concern monasteries as lamas and chomos. They works for the monateries cultivate lands, rared animals and look after their forests. On the other side low population unable to cultive more land, therefore land holding was low, Agriculture production was also low. Besides every household had to give annual

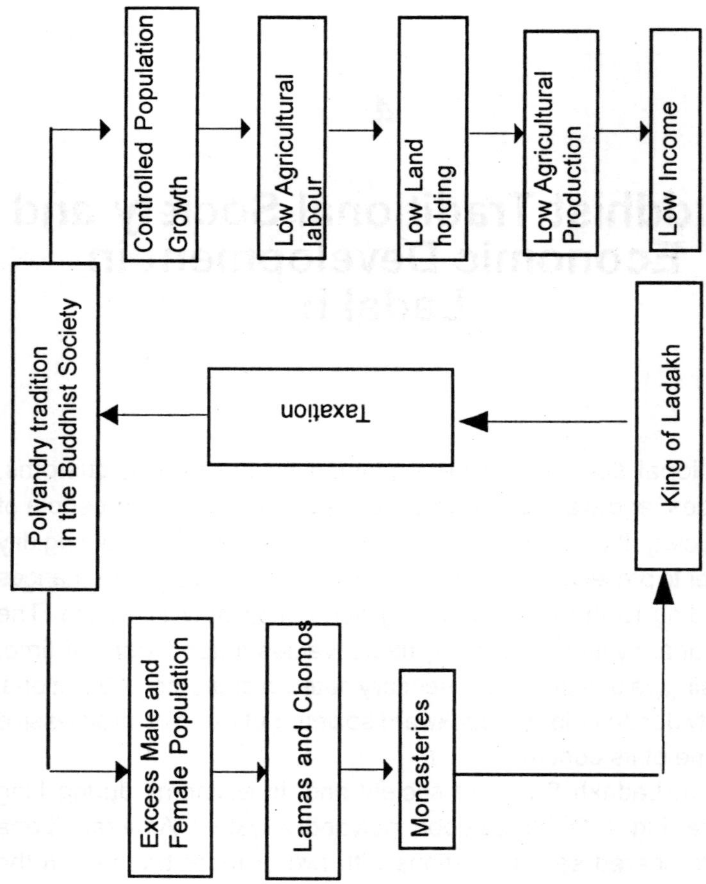

Fig. 4.1. Economy of traditional Buddhist Society during king regime.

land revenue tax in kind. This caused the poor economic condition of Ladakhi Buddhists.

After 1947 Ladakh became a part of India, therefore to protect ladakh from enemies Indian defence invested money for the infrastructure development. The excess labours got chance to get employment in building roads. Then the Ladakhi Buddhist society got some external push because of temporary earning, hence a slight change had been noticed (Fig. 4.2.)

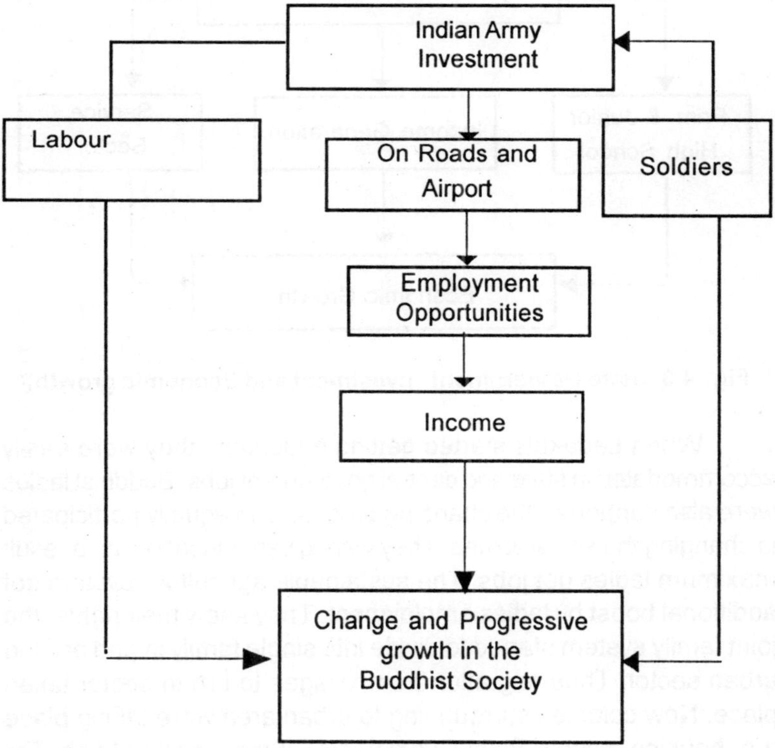

Fig. 4.2 : Change and Progressive growth in the Buddhist Society of Ladakh after 1947.

Gradually state government also started to open its departments in ladakh region. Initially Kashmiri employees were sent to Ladakh on deputation. They usually pass their time in Ladakh.

Thus the state government didn't find any positive return. Therefore, government decided to educate ladakhis so that at least clerical works might be easily solved. As a result many Junior High Schools and Primary schools were opened. Ladakhi Buddhists under government policy sent their children to government schools. Thus with the education, social rigity viz. Polyandry system started breaking and economic growth had taken place (Fig. 4.3.)

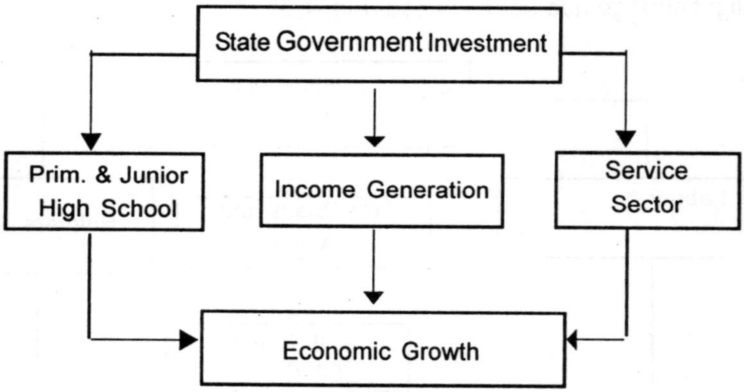

Fig. 4.3: State Govternment investment and Economic growth.

When Ladakhis started getting education, they were easily accommodated in state and central government jobs. Buddhist ladies were also supported the changing process and equally participated in changing the social values. They were given education, as a result maximum ladies got jobs. The sustainable agriculture system got additional boost by ladies employment. They knew their rights, the joint family system started to divide into single family in and around urban sector. Thus migration from villages to urban sector taken place. New colonies surrounding to urban area were taking place e.g. housing colony, Tashi Gyatsal, etc. at the vicinity of Leh (Fig 4.4).

The per capita income overall slightly increased in the region. However, unequal income distribution divided the community in two groups—Rich and poor. A small group enjoyed higher standard of life, in the colonies wine shops swelled to meet demands for those who have money in their pockets. In the rural sector the economy had accompanied the following characteristics.

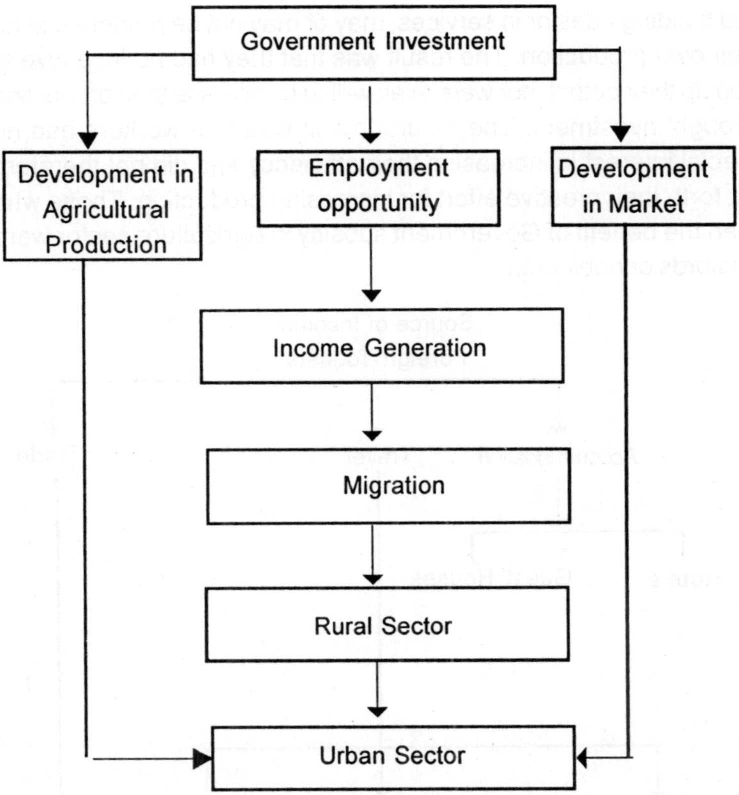

Fig. 4.4: Women Empowerment and Migration Cycle between Rural to Urban Sector.

(1) Agriculture still remain the most economic activity. However, vegetable cultivation being encouraged. Villagers started to sale vegetable production to Army supply.

(2) Cottage industries continued to produce to meet agriculture low-value goods demand e.g. baskets, threading items etc.

(3) Methods of production followed to be traditional and largely primitive.

(4) Implements used remained simple and power used by mainly human and animal.

The economy described above was accompanied by a society divided into classes, e.g. actual workers, whether on land or road and building rides or in services, may or may not be responsible for their own production. The result was that they had no incentive to step up their output, nor were even willing to increase their production through investment. The natural result was that workers had no special interest in increasing their efficiency and did not therefore put forth their creative effort for increasing production. Those who used the benefit of Government subsidy in Agriculture sector were landlords or noblemen.

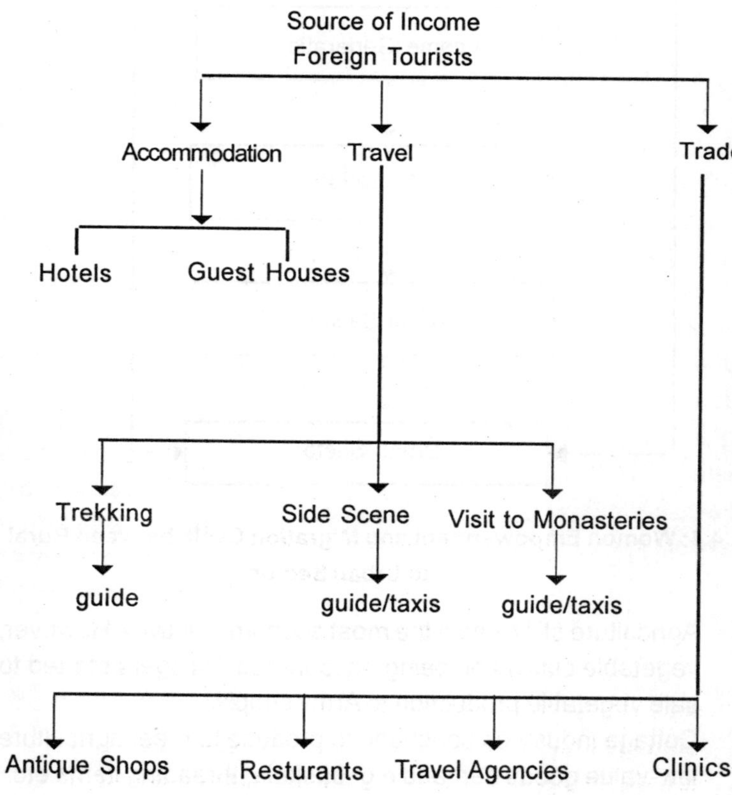

Fig. 4.5 : Tourism based economy in Ladakh.

After summer 1974 foreigners started to visit Ladakh as Jammu & Kashmir open bar for them. Within one decade the flux of foreigners in Leh town increased up to 25,000. As a result many Guest Houses, Hotels, Travel Agencies, Restaurants, Antique Shops etc. had taken place. Tourism treated as industry. In Government level subsidies were given for the construction of hotels, Guest Houses etc. Consequently bulk of labour was required to meet the demand, They imported them from Bihar, Orissa, Madhya Pradesh, Nepal etc. Thus economy is urban sector taking up its position for development. The Rural sector was also considered by the state Government; various schemes were launched in order to increase agricultural production viz. to supply N.P.K. fertilizer in subsidy rates (Fig. 4.5).

In urban sector the living standard has been increased. Ladakhis now started to construct cemented buildings and each household has T.V., Radio, Telephone, car etc. They very well awared about their identity, hence under Ladakh Buddhist Association started agitation for Scheduled Tribes and U.T. Status to Ladakh. Central Government accepted their maximum demands. Leh and Kargil were given Autonomous Hill Councils and allotted separate funds for their infrastructure development.

Today both Kargil and Leh districts under the umbrella of Hill Councils are getting fast economic development. Religiously both Buddhist and Muslim communities are very well aware of their religious monuments and culture. Number of NGOs are being registered in this line. They have been approached to state, Central and world financial institutions for funding. Many of them got success. Now under Desert Development Agency, number of village societies are given funds for the construction of water shed. Thus through this, irrigation development activities are taking place. Subsidies are given for the improvement of livestock, milk production has been increased. As a result the traditional Buddhist society in Ladakh fastly changed into progressive society in which they are able to increase their agricultural as well as milk production. Thus income is also started to generate and hence economic growth in this sector is also being noticed. At the vicinity of Leh and other neighbouring villages, during cultivation and cropping seasons they felt acute agriculture labour shortage. Nepali and Doda labours are being therefore employed and some time given them land on contract (Fig. 4.6).

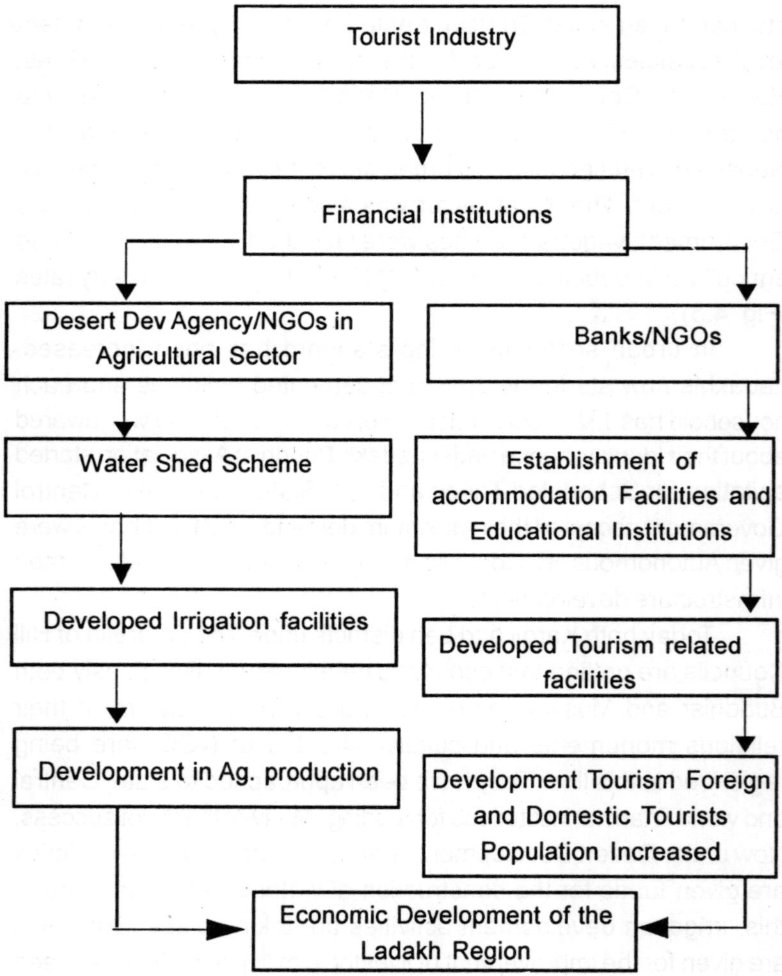

Fig. 4.6 : Tourism and Economic Devlopment of the Ladakh Region.

In conclusion, rural and urban sectors of Ladakh have come under the perview of economic development. Lamas have major role to intact Buddhist population towards their tradition, however people who are trained through scientific lines help in economic development activities.

5

A Study of Drinking Water Supply in Leh District

The major source of water supply in Ladakh is Indus and its tributaries. Besides lakes are the alternative source of water. The Panggong Tso, Thomoriri and Tso Kar have no outlet, hence are highly brakish. The Yaye Tso, Kium Tso etc. on the other hand are fresh water lakes.

In Leh district raw water is not admissible for drinking purpose. Pipe and ground water have bacteriologically satisfactory for this purpose (Table 5.1).

Table 5.1 reveals that –

1. Water supply through pipe is 58 per cent satisfactory and can be used for drinking purpose.
2. Spring, stream and river water is unsatisfactory and should not be used for drinking purpose.
3. Frozen water can be used for drinking purpose.

The bacteriological quality of water faecal coliform/100 ml < 1 was recorded between 12 to 13 per cent of raw stream and spring water; whereas it had more than 50 per cent in pipe supply water and in frozen water and tubewell was having in between 67 to 100 per cent. The following Table 5.2 shows the details.

Table 5.1

Summary of Bacteriological Analysis of Drinking Water Showing Prevalence of Contamination in Ladakh

Piped	19	11 (57.89)	3 (15.79)	15 (26.32)
Tube Wall	02	02	-	-
Hand Pump	02	-	01	011
Spring	15	01	03	11
Stream	26	01	01	(73.33) 23
Frogen Water	03	03	-	(88.46) -
River	04	-	-	04
Total	71	18 (25.35)	8 (11.27)	45 (63.38)

Parenthesis represents %.

Source : Drinking water quality Leh district (Ladakh) Jammu & Kashmir, National Mission on Drinking Water in villages, National Mission Programme, Government of India, Industrial Toxicolgy Research Centre, Lucknow, 1988 : 12.

Table 5.2

Summary of Bacteriological Analysis of Drinking Water Showing Prevalence of Contamination

Sl.No.	*Source*	*No. of Sample*	*Faecal Coliform 100 ml <1*
1.	Piped Supply	19	10 (52.63)
2.	Tube Wall	02	02
3.	Hand Pump	02	-

(Contd.)

(Contd.)

Sl.No.	*Source*	*No. of Sample*	*Faecal Coliform 100 ml <1*
4.	Spring	15	02 (13.33)
5.	Stream	26	03 (11.54)
6.	Frogen Water	03	02
8.	River	04	-
	Total	71	19 (26.7)

Parenthesis represents %.

Source : Drinking water quality Leh district (Ladakh) Jammu & Kashmir, National Mission on Drinking Water in villages , op. cit., p. 12.

The presence of faecal type coliforms such as Salmonella typhi, organism causing cholera, diarrhoea and gastroenteritis or hapatities vitus. The following table 5.3 shows that during 1983-87 some deaths were recorded by using the contaminated water, when water source purified by chlorination no deaths were noticed.

The presence of nitrate may cause cancer particulaly where breast feeding is common. But in Leh district because of less use of chemical fertilizers nitrate level is much lower than the danger level. Similarly presence of calcium, iron and sulphate is also lower than the highest desirable level. Thus no danger for health from iron bacteria as concentration 0.05 mg/ litre is considered satisfactory. Similarly there is no harm from pesticides, farmers use the same in a very less quantity) (Appendix 5.1 to 5.4)

In conclusion I would say tubewell, pipe supply and frozen water safe for health. In villages spring water after chlorination can be used for drinking purpose.

Table 5.3

Statement showing the water borne disease in Leh district (Excluding SNM Hospital Leh)

Year/	*Polio*		*Entric fever*		*Gastroentrities*		*Viral Hapetitis*		*Cholera*	
	No. of cases	*No. of deaths*	*No. of cases*	*No. of deaths*	*No. of cases*	*No. of deaths*	*No. of cases*	*No. of deaths*	*No. of cases*	*No. of deaths*
1983-84	-	-	17	02	971	01	23	02	-	-
1984-85	-	-	10	01	1516	02	15	03	-	-
1985-86	-	-	13	-	1746	03	07	01	-	-
1986-87	-	-	18	-	1609	02	21	-	-	-
1987-88	-	-	06	-	2459	-	-	-	52	-

Appendix -5.1
Metal Analysis of Drinking Water in Leh District

Block	*Village*	*Source*	*Source Name*	*Fe Ug./ml*	*Ca Ug./ml*
Durbuk	Durbuk	Spring	-	0.421	46.157
"	Cashukul	Stream	-	0.067	15.857
"	Thurak	"	-	0.132	25.357
Khalsi	Gheramangagu	Spring	-	0.055	06.697
"	Larddo	"	-	0.169	22.557
"	Housing	Stream	-	0.433	14.417
"	Colony				
"	Timasgam	"	Timasgam	0.587	08.777
"	Bema	Spring	-	0.221	27.557
"	Tar-Hipti	"	-	0.445	21.357
"	Dumkar Gongma	"	-	0.197	17.597
"	Basgo	" (PS) Yougma	Spang	0.237	26.957
"	Achinathang	" (PS)	-	-	-
"	Basgo Thankok	Stream	Basgo Nala	0.741	09.197
"	Nurla	"	-	0.473	05.717
"	Ney	"	-	1.255	32.957
"	Dumkhar	Spring (PS)	-	0.201	06.917
"	Likir	Stream	Likir	0.839	07.577
"	Khalsi	Spring (PS)	-	0.116	20.157
"	Saspol	"(PS)	Spanktik	0.143	05.417
"	Kurmarik	"	-	0.083	09.037
"	Alchi	"(PS)	-	0.136	15.757
"	Da	"	-	0.249	15.777
"	Rizong Gonpa	"	-	0.091	48.557

Source : Op.cit.: 43.
Ps - Piped Supply

Appendix - 5.2
Chemical Analysis of Drinking Water in Leh District

Block	*Village*	*Source*	*Source Name*	*Hardness mg/L*	*SO_4 mg/L*	*NO_3 mg/L*
Durbuck	Durbuck	Spring	-	164.0	22.40	0.035
"	Cashukul	Stream	-	60.0	07.00	ND
"	Thurak	"	-	96.0	07.00	"
Khalri	Gheramango	Spring	-	80.0	12.40	0.050
"	Laddo	"	-	92.0	12.00	ND
"	Housing Colony	Stream	-	56.0	03.45	"
"	Timasgam	"	Timasgam	32.0	02.75	"
"	Barma	"	-	24.0	02.05	0.050
"	Tar-Hipti	"	-	100.0	11.0	0.230
"	Dumkar	"	-	64.0	04.20	ND
	Gongma	-	-	-	-	-

(Contd.)

(Contd.)

Block	*Village*	*Source*	*Source Name*	*Hardness mg/L*	*So_4 mg/L*	*NO_3 mg/L*
"	Basgo	" (PS)	Spang Yougma	80.0	22.00	0.250
"	Achinathang	" (PS)	-	44.0	06.20	ND
"	Basgo Thankok	Stream	Basgo Nala	32.0	12.40	0.100
"	Nurla	"	-	28.0	02.75	0.035
"	Ney	"	-	112.0	22.40	0.300
"	Dumkar	Spring (PS)	-	32.0	02.70	0.035
"	Likir	Stream	Likir	24.0	11.20	0.400
"	Khalsi	Spring (PS)	-	88.0	05.50	ND
"	Saspol	" (PS)	Spanktik	28.0	12.40	0.360
"	Kurmarik	"	-	36.0	02.05	ND
"	Alchi	" (PS)	-	64.0	15.20	0.500
"	Da	"	-	112.0	27.50	0.015
"	Rizong Gonpa	"	-	196.0	15.20	0.170

Source : Drinking water qulity Leh District (Ladakh) J & K, National Mission on Drinking Water in Villages, Industrial Toxicology Research Centre, Lucknow, 1988; Report : 36.

Appendix - 5.3
Chemical Analysis of Drinking Water in Leh District

Block	*Village*	*Source*	*Source Name*	*Hardness mg/L*	*SO_4 mg/L*	*NO_3 mg/L*
Leh	Karzoo	Stream	Shyldan	44.0	07.00	0.100
"	Leh (town)	River	Indus	80.0	11.00	0.300
"	Choglamsar	River (PS)	"	48.0	07.00	0.050
"	Gyarong	Spring	Gaylung	64.0	08.30	ND
"	Ranbirpura	River	Indus	60.0	21.00	0.100
"	Leh & Shankar	OW	Shankar	64.0	04.20	0.20
"	Changra	Spring (PS)	-	100.0	11.20	ND
"	Shara	Stream	-	60.0	03.40	0.035
"	Ganglas & Leh town	OW (PS)	T-Trench	88.0	05.50	0.065
"	Giaya	Stream	-	60.0	08.30	0.035
"	Karzoo	Spring	Karzoo	72.0	04.20	ND
"	karzoo	H.P.	-	72.0	05.50	0.33
"	Lamdan School	Spring (PS)	Skamlung	160.0	70.00	0.035

(Contd.)

(Contd.)

Block	*Village*	*Source*	*Source Name*	*Hardness mg/L*	*So_4 mg/L*	*NO_3 mg/L*
Leh	Upsi, Giya meru	Stream	-	60.0	08.30	0.035
"	Spituk	Spring	spituk	112.0	07.00	0.17
Nubra	Diskit	Stream	-	56.0	02.75	ND
"	Charasa	"	-	60.0	14.00	"
"	Pratapur	"	-	60.0	02.75	"
"	Skampuk	"	-	60.0	04.20	"
"	Tiger	"	-	52.0	02.75	"
"	Panamic	"	-	56.0	05.40	"
"	Hunder	"	-	60.0	02.75	"

Source : Op.cit.: 42.
PS- Piped Supply
OW - Oozed water
ND - Not detectable

Appendix - 5.4
Metal Analysis of Drinking Water in Leh District

Block	*Village*	*Source*	*Source Name*	*Fe ug/L*	*Ca_4 ug/L*
Leh	Karzoo	Stream	Shyldan	0.42	11.75
"	Leh (town)	River	Indus	12.46	30.0
"	Choglamgar	-	"	01.2	13.14
"	Gyarong	Spring	Gaylang	00.74	18.88
"	Ranbirpura	River	Indus	07.56	23.16
"	Shankar	OW	Shankar	0.36	19.44
"	Changra	Spring (PS)	-	0.20	22.56
"	Shara	Stream	-	0.31	11.84
"	Ganglas	OW (PS)	Trench	0.30	22.56
"	Giaya	Stream	-	0.12	13.78
"	Karzoo	Spring	Karzoo	02.08	16.14
"	karzoo	H.P.	-	0.50	13.86
"	Lamdan School	Spring (PS)	Skamlung	03.10	57.38
"	Upsi, Giya Meru	Stream	-	0.26	12.84
"	Spituk	Spring	Spituk	0.30	37.76
Nubra	Diskit	Stream	-	0.06	11.38
"	Charasa	"	-	0.92	36.76
"	Pratapur	"	-	0.04	11.86
"	Skampuk	"	-	0.04	13.42
"	Tiger	"	-	0.06	13.26
"	Panamic	"	-	0.02	11.96
"	Hunder	"	-	0.22	12.62
"	Khargang	"	-	0.14	12.72

Source : Op.cit.: 43.
PS- Piped Supply
OW - Oozed water
ND - Not detectable

6

Losar : A New Year Festival of Ladakh and its Neighbouring Regions

Losar is among the important festivals of Himalaya. It is celebrated by Buddhists as New Year festival, preceded by the number of preparatory ceremonies wind up the old year and begin the new year with the hope that the new year will be better than the old, perhaps to fulfil two aims together : to chase away the evil elements that hover all around and of inspiring faith in the future. It is also necessary to say that there should be no remains of anything evil, unlucky or sinful from the previous year may follow, and in the following year people will get happiness in their life. Thus everything must begin a new, in peace and tranquility, and all that maybe even indirectly unlucky must be carefully avoided.[1]

In Tibet Losar feast begins on the 29th of the last month of the year according to the Tibetan calandar. On this occasion people collect some soots and place them in a stone jar with a black edge, then throw on a crossroads. By doing so they belief that all the evil spirits from their house get out with soots in different directs. Sometimes they throw rags, black seeds and some money with the soots as if to placate the hostile forces and by off the calamities that they can cause. At the same time they also purify their kitchen.

It is said that in kitchen *Thaplha* or hearth god resides, he protects the house, any impurity may sully his dwelling place.He is sensitive, therefore, such impurity may harm the welfare of family.[2]

In the dinner feast masters and servants of the house sit together. A soup called *Thukpa* is made of meat, cheese and vegetables and has dumplings in it. Strange token or objects are hidden in the dumplings to reveal the character of person 'receiving them'. A person who gets pea in the middle of the dumplings represents the qualities of frugality or stinginess. A piece of paper if he gets in the dumplings, indicates that the person could be blown about by the wind like paper with no opinion of his own. Salt indicates that the recipient is not outgoing but know his own worth, and a twisted piece of string indicates that the person enjoy gossiping. Thus everyone is expected to drink nine bowels of heavy soup for good luck. In the course of the evening's celebration, two dough figures representing a man and woman are paraded through the house, when they have made the complete tour of the rooms, are thrown out of the window. They represented the passing year's bad luck. The whole gathering applude and cheer as they get out the window. At 3 o'clock in the morning of the New Year's day, the entire households would get of bed and go to the family chapel or shrine for prayer, the elders lead, followed by children then eat a bowl wheat porridge for good luck.[3]

Tibetans in Lhasa used to go to the Jo-khang, wear new cloths, offer prayers in Jo-khang, return to home; later set firecrackers.[4]

Losar is celebrated in winter by the inhabitants of Indus belt from Kailash onwards. It is of course the function to attend the computation of time. However, who commits the precious seed to bosom of mother earth, hopes for wealth from the harvest and happiness for himself and his family. The similar custom is followed by the inhabitants of Gilgit, Hunza and Nagar, where the head of the community on an auspicious day, sows, in the first furrow some gold-dust in the hope that it will bring a bumper crop of golden wheat and barley. Finally, after having bumper crop production leads to celebrate Lo-sar to bring happiness in the family.[5]

Lo-sar as a New Year festival is celebrated by Japanese, Bhutanese and even Buddhists of South-East Asian countries during spring season which generally falls in between February and March.[6]

The people of ancient Zhang-Zhung from Kailash to Dardistan celebrate Lo-sar in the mid winter (i.e., in December or January) depending upon the prescribed local calendar.[7]

The inhabitants who live in between Brahmaputra valley and China celebrate the same during spring (i.e., in between February and March).

In Baltistan it is celebrated by Muslims as 'Nau-Roz' or New Year festival during 21/22 March every year.[8]

In Cang-Thangand nomads of Tibet calculate the date of Lo-sar according to the sun position. S.S. Gergan remarks :

"In the case of nomads who live almost exclusively on the produce of their livestock, the year is divided significantly into two : (i) that which livestock can seek their food on open pasture land, (ii) that which they have to be sheltered from the inclemency of the weather in caves, in the safely of open pens or stalls. The nomads of Tibet and Cang-Thang are guided by twenty-eight constellations, the principal stars, the months in which they are visible in the northern horizon, their course, and time of disappearence. They change their grazing areas and community camps according to the calendar indicated by the constellations. The agriculturists in the Indus valley also have an accurate knowledge of the movements of the stars. Their agriculture calendar includes the irrigation of fallow lands, soil working,clog breaking, sowing, harvesting alpine grass for hay, barley and wheat. Each nomad camp has its own local indicator, a peak or peaks used as a kind of sundial to denote the movement of the stars, moon and the sun at a particular time of the year. In the Kailash-Mansarovar area, the majestic peak of Kailash is the indicator defining the change in the sun's and moon's course, from the winter solastic to the vernal equinox, and to the summer solastic. The Kailash-Mansarovar and the Mayum-La watershed between the Indus and Brahmaputra forms an ancient demarcation of ethnic groups. The people living in the region to the north of the Brahmaputra valley and the people inhabiting the southern side of the Kailash and Mayum-la, differ in the calculation of their Lo-sar dates. Those belonging to the southern side of Kailash – Mansarovar, the valley of the Indus and Sutlej rivers calculate their Lo-sar at the time the sun begins its northward journey, i.e., December, coinciding with the Margashirsha, Shukla Pratipad, as observed in the days of Mahabharata."[9]

In Lahul, Buddhists before celebrating Lo-sar festival, come out from their respective house with *mashal*,[10] in evening gathered at an assigned place. Thereafter carry the same together and throw outside the village. On return home, when find their houses are closed, they requested :

"To open the door."

"What have you been brought?"

"Sergi kau khyong i.e. I brought '*kau*' made of gold for you."

In this way with his family celebrate Lo-sar festival happily and get out the evil spirits from his house by throwing mashal outside the house. In Ladakh Lo-sar is celebrated 25th of 10th month of the year. According to the Tibetan calendar, Ladakhi Buddhists celebrate Lo-sar two months earlier than Tibetans. The reasons behind are :

1. It was studied that generally Lo-sar concides with the birthday of Tsong-khapa, the founder of Gelukpa order of Mahayana Buddhism. It is believed that Tsong-khapa was born and got parinirvana at the same date. Therefore, lamas of the Gelukpa monasteries celebrate Tsong-khapa's birthday as 'Galdan lang chot'.[11] On the eve of this festival lamas offer 'chot-pas', chant 35 Buddhas mantra, lit lamps before the deities and lighted the monasteries like *Deepawali*. On this occasion they read Tsong-khapa's pothis and promise to follow his teachings in their life. On the other hand laymen celebrate this with Lo-sar. On this day they eat meat, drink chhang and marry. This way encouraged animal killing and intoxication habit in the society. Hence, on the Tsong-khapa's birthday to stop such evils Ladakhis unanimously decided to celebrate Lo-sar after Tsong-khapa birthday.
2. It is said that when King Jamyang Namgyal decided to go with his army to Purig to face Balti army; his advisors and representatives of various villages of Ladakh met him and requested to celebrate Lo-sar earlier, as it would be good for him and his army. King did the same, later it became the tradition.[12]

3. In olden days Ladakhis celebrate this festival during autumn season, as people became happy to see their harvested crops. So after cutting and thrashing their crops they make sattu and chhang. Thus, invite their relatives and enjoy their rest time happily. But later they thought if such practice would continue they could neither attend Dun, Dagang, Pakston etc. ceremonies nor the annual festivals of all big monasteries.

Thus, the date of Lo-sar festival shifted in such manner that they could celebrate social ceremonies as well as to attend the monastery festivals.

Lo-sar Festival in Ladakh :

In the central Ladakh Ladakhi Buddhist arrange dinner feast in which all the relatives are invited. This time a special Thukpa is served. It is made of meat, dry paneer (dry cheese called Churpe), vegetables, pea and has dumplings in it. Strange tokens which are hidden in the dumplings reveal the character of the person.

The details of strange tokens hidden in dumplings are :

1. A piece of religious text paper 2. A image of sun made by flour 3. A small piece of wood nature 4. White hair	These are the symbol of good nature
5. *Yar Gyuks and Mar Gyuks* ? (something passes through hole) 6. Je-ma-ring-go (chilli) 7. Coal 8. Gokpa (or garlic) 9. Salt	These are the symbol of bad nature

In some other parts of Ladakh the following nine objects are hidden in dumplings :

1. Coal
2. Salt
3. Chilli
4. Sun image made of flour ?
5. Moon image made of flour?
6. Agarbatti?
7. Sugar

8. Semarango ?
9. Black hair

Before taking Thukpa, all members of the family and relatives decided what have they do for their entertainment? For example if any member has coal, semarango etc. in his bowl, he will be punished by others, if has image of sun or moon he will be given gifts.

In Leh and its surrounding a person who has coal in his bowl have to say 5 to 10 times *chag-tsal* to all the sitting members; who has sun or moon image presented some money (i.e., Rs. 50 to Rs. 150 depending upon status); in case a person has chilli, he is supposed to be talkative or may have abusing nature. Who have coal, his nature to criticize others; who has sugar, always speak sweet or polite; who has semarango, would be yes man of his boss; if salt comes, means lazy and on *Agarbatti,* means well behaved. In brief during the dinner feast all the family members enjoy the party by giving light punishment to those who have coal, salt etc. in their bowls and tease them by saying you have black heart or *spoon feeder,* etc.

On the 30th people at the early morning go to the cremation ground lit lamps and offer dry fruits, i.e., apple, apricots etc. to their relatives' grave. In evening they divide into two parties and say to each other as :

"Those who are enemy and do not possess good thoughts, may destroy in this *mashals;* let's together hope for the better future in this new year."

Both the parties then throw *mashals* outside the village and return to their respective houses. In house they take a portion from the cooked food and put some pieces of it on '*ka*',[13] '*zot*',[14] '*chotkhung*'[15] and '*Tangra*'[16]. Thereafter, all family member go to 'chotkhang' for prayer. On this occasion family members are expected to present those who do not return home some or the other reason, they also pray for their good future.

In Nubra, on Namgang people make flour skying, put them in row on the almirah where old, new, small and big utensils are placed. This time they prey (or *stendel*) for the welfare of all family members. On 1st of the 11th month of the Tibetan calendar all children and other members of the family wear new cloths and go to the village temple, offer sweets etc. to Buddha statue and pray for their happy life. They clean their houses and the surroundings, hung *tarcoks*[17] at their house's roof, thereafter take food and go to their relative houses, pay their regards to elders, who in returns give them chag'zen[18] or good food items. This trend continues till 15th of the month.

On 11th villagers celebrate cuk-cik; on this occasion people divided in various groups among them become *Abi & Meme*[19]. They paint their faces like *Abi & Meme* (i.e., old man and woman), wear dress accordingly; go each villeger's house with their groups and ask them to give flour, money etc. on the eve of Lo-sar. At the late evening they eat drink and marry.

On 29 th, people divided in groups make Thukpa and serve to the villagers whoever pass through, it is called *Srang-thug.*[20] In evening they gather at one place, carry *mashals* and throw the same together, say Co-Bumskyang[21] died, he is no more. Later join dinner feat, *thukpa* is served, in which coal, chilli, onion, hair, salt etc objects are hidden; who has coal in his bowl , say his mind is black like coal; on chilli - he will be talkative, on onion - he seems to be poor; sheep hair indicates the man will be rich and salt means, he doesn't stand at one place.

In Da-Bima, villagers lit *mashals* and sing the following song:

"Shekyang serika seri co ce yot,
Vay vay mala ne nang pan me chu,
Pan me jera nga sang sam sang zik."

Mostly Ladakhis make skying,[22] on 29th and decorate them at their kitchen almirah.[23] In some places they make skying on 7-9 of the 11th month on 29-30 0ffer *khura* to their *Ishta deva* and pray for their good future. Normally 10-15 villagers have common *Ishta deva*; they pray together, lit lamps. It is called *lha-sol* (Tib. lha-gsol).

On first of the 11th month all brothers and sisters of the family go to meet father and mother, pay their regards and wish them for long and happy life and offer them *khadags*. This tradition is called *ches-chak. Khadags* are not offered to pregnant ladies as people belief that it is not good in their tradition.[24]

In some villages people on the full moon carry breads to their respective house and throw them from roof in different directions after making half surface black.

In other villages people during dark night shoot arrows. They take skying to their respective house, break it into pieces and from roof throw them to different directions, while shooting arrows, they say; "*tse tse*" (Tib. tse tse co srol yod). They do this on 3rd of 11th month, it means may they live long.

In Shyam side particularly in Nimo, Tia and Timosgam; villagers on the first day of the said month take chhang, breads etc. to their friends and relatives, pay regards to elders and love to youngers. It is called *chabjan*, it continues for five days. From 2nd to 4th day children of the village go to each house and ask , "Please give us some pieces of wood", when they are taken so become happy and say, "chil-chil". The details is cited below:

"'Aa ma le 'ju,
'A pha le 'ju,
'chil 'chil mo,
chal chal mo,
'ma le 'ju,
'ma le 'ju,
bsal na bsal,
ma bsal na ma bsal,
Aa ma le bsal,
ju bsal len,
dgong pa bsal."

On 6th and 7th day, they take lhato in the middle of a plain, lit firewoods at the surrounding of it, eat, drink and enjoy by dancing and singing different songs with the tune of surna and Daman which is played by the Mon and Gara[25] of the village.

In Tia, villagers make *Torma*[26] by *sattu*[27], throw it either at the inn, where three paths meet or outside the village. On 3rd, they take half black breads to their house roofs and throw them to different directions by saying the following words :

"lo gsar la sus he le,
lo bzang sus te lo ngan
skyur te,
tse tse."[28]

On first of the 11th month upto 3rd, Ladakhis make *lhato spoces*; on this occasion a group of phasphuns[29] gather on the roof of any one family's house. They change the cloths of Ishta deva and pray together.

On 3rd in Nurla, 4th in Timasgyam and 5th day in Tia, villagers celebrate *sta-gyus.*[30] On this occasion they bring their horses at plain. Lardak,[31] at first rider runs fast to the demarcated point, later return to his origin position; similarly others follow. At the centre of plain a target is made by sand. All participants on their turn shoot arrow after riding on their respective horses with full speed, if one hits the target, he has to arrange Lo-sar feast for others. Sometimes, they run from the demarcated line and throw stones to the target, where one bread is placed, if one hits the target, he has to arrange feast for others.

In 'Tia' village during Lo-sar villagers make '*Aa ba Guru*' or '*Lama Jugu*'.[32] On this occasion one man outside the village wears devil's dress, called "*Aa ba Guru*", carries "Torma" [33] and "*Khadags*',[34] others follow him and say "*Hop pala hop seri pholong.*"[35] Later '*Aa ba Guru*' put '*torma*' and '*Kangs*' on a big stone and, start dancing with *daman*,[36] villagers gather here to see '*Aa ba Guru*' dance. In evening when function is finished, '*Aa ba Guru*' takes *torma* and throw it at inn.

In Da village, two villagers wearmasks of *Abi & Meme* after morning bath, drink apricot oil, by 11 o'clock along with village children go each house, who offer them chhang, sattu etc. In response they say '*Losar la Tashis deleks - July*[37] and sing the following songs.

Lu gu bali kangce shar pute Jok,
Ache Ogme samte cak kho le Jok,
Phili go na nang go ang dang se Jok,
Curu mari dimbu dim khang se Jok.

In Chusod Yogma and Choglamsar villagers celebrate Abi & *Meme* function on 5th of the 11th month. On this occasion *Abi & Meme* at first take bath in morning, wear old man and woman dress and masks. Then come at a big room where musicians play daman with lar-nga, *Pheps-nga*, skyod-nga, people dance and sing songs. Thereafter, they go house to house with *Abi-Meme*, do the same, eat and drink *chhang*.

In Timasgam, *Abi-Meme* celebrate on 3rd of the 11th month. On the same day at Timargam palace, villagers organise a function in which they sing songs, dance and share joks. Two people sit on artificial skins and dance. At last one man set fire crackers and kill the skyings, with this the function comes to an end.

In Hemis Shukpacan, villagers on this day make *Te-thap*[38]. Two men wear black and white dress and play with swords. At the end white dresssed man kill the black dressed man by his sword. This indicates black dressed man, symbol of evil spirits killed by good spirit, thus in the following year evil spirits would not harm anyone.

In Basgo, during olden days people gathered at the field in front of the king Namgyal's palace. In the mid field a effigy of a skying was made. At first *Kharpon*[39] ride on his horse, run towards skying and tried to pick up, then *Lhardan* did the same, thereafter villagers followed this, who succeed in this game was offered *khadags* by every participants and welcomed him in the evening function, in which people sat in tents sing *langpo, chikpa, chakspe, chosgang, yangskyit* etc. People with folk songs and daman and *surma* music dance *kompa sumsek.*[40] At late night when king ordered to stop dance, the villagers payed their regards to king by saying *Julley-Julley* and returned to their houses.

In Chang-thang people celebrate Lo-sar from 29th evening of 10th month. They make *Thukpa* in which meat, churpe, pea etc. put in for good taste. Thereafter, family members wear good cloths and clean every room, even *chot-khang.*[41]

In house temple they put *chot-pa*, *skying,* etc. Next day lama is invited for *puja*. On this day kitchen room is decorated. As soon as lama completes his *puja*, he comes to the kitchen,where Thukpa is served to him alongwith *Aa-ba,*[42] *Aa-ma*[43] and other elders of the family. The youngers help in serving *Thukpa.*[44] Generally young girls serve *thukpa*. On 9th of 11th month youngers get up early in the morning, pay their regards to elders and say *'Tashidaleks'.*[45] They go to their relatives and do the same, at home offer *chhang* to the guests; thereafter all gather at one place and arrange a function in which they dance *Jabro*[46] with local music. Elders on this day go to the monasteries, say 'Tashi daleks' to lamas who in return offer *chhang*[47] or tea. Later they come to a field where horse race is organised.

Lo-sar *chhang* has special importance, when married women go to their house to say Jally or *'Tashi daleks'* offer *chhang* to them and sing the following song :

"di ring jagpo Lo-sar re jak,
chang nang Lo-sar re pung pa skyot,
di ring re jaspo tashis se jak,
changma nang tashis daleks jug shik."

Translation
"Today is Lo-sar day,
All go to drink chhang in the eve of Lo-sar,
Today is an auspicious day
We welcome you all."

In conclusion Lo-sar, begins after the birthday celebration of Tsong Khapa, the founder of Geluk pa order. Gonpas, therefore, first illuminated, thereafter public illuminate their houses with small mustered oil lamps. *Me-to* is made by bundles of willow and junifer branches, after liting, *Me-to* looks like burning torches, which are being carried outside the villages, then throw away together. They belief that with the *Me-to* all evil spirits get out from the village. In some villages boys indulge in mock fighting, they dress up as old man and woman and wear their masks. Children also enjoy by burning dried grass.

On this occasion each household replace *Lhato*, which is placed on the roof of chot-khang, family members offer pray before the *Isht dev.* The male family members on 'Me-sol' go to the cremation ground, light up lamps and offer food and drinks to their deceased relatives. In dinner feast special *thukpa* is served with various dumplings which are the symbol of good and bad characters. Through these all the family members and relatives enjoy the feast.

In the countryside of Ladakh various functions are organized by the villagers. In some villages horse races and archery competition are organized, the winners on these events are offered khadags and chhang. Besides, people in some villages divided in groups, among them two dress up in *'Lama-Zigu'* and perform certain rites at all houses in the village to drive away evils.

The female also come out from their respective houses in an open field, sing songs, dance with male, and enjoy Lo-sar festival by saying good bye to social evils and welcome the new year with the hope of their good future.

Musical Instruments used during Lo-sar in Darchiks Village:

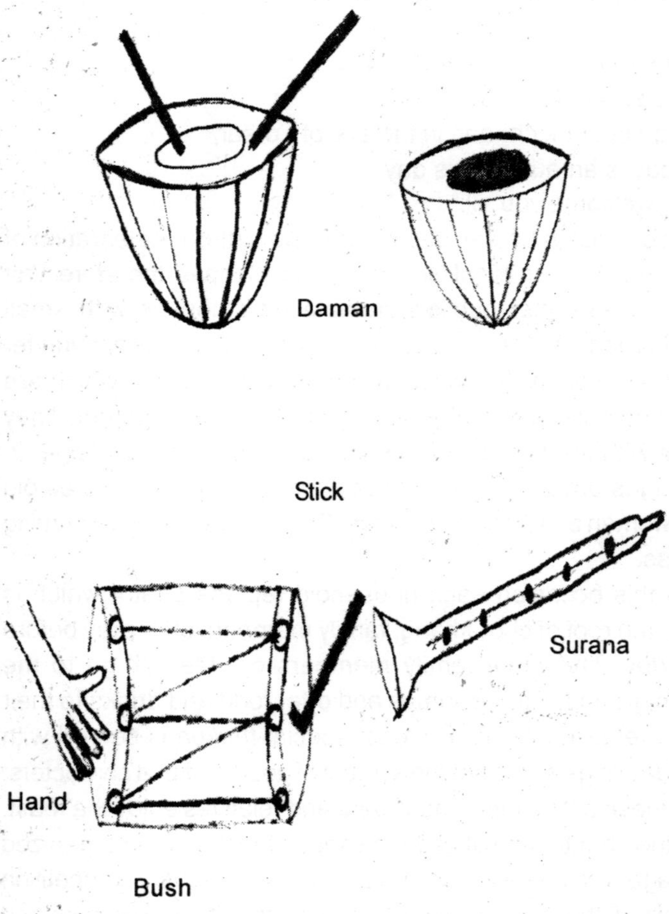

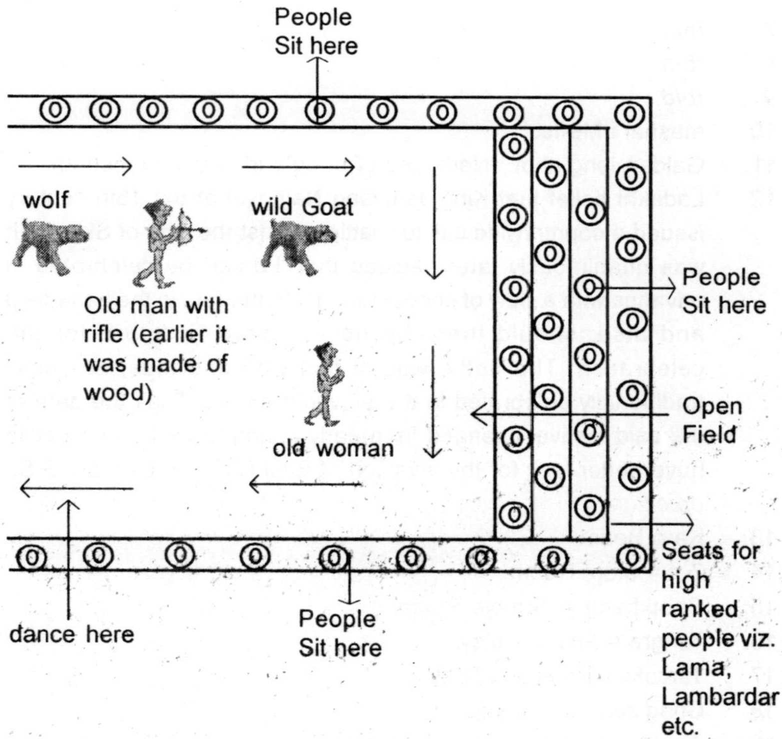

Figure- 6.1

Old Man and Woman Dance with Wild Goat and Wolf in Darchiks Village during Losar Festival

Notes and References

1. Tucci, Giuseppe : 'Tibet : Lands of Snow', Tr. J.E. Stapleton Driver; Oxford Univ. Pub.; New Delhi, 1973 : 144.
2. *Ibid.* 147.
3. Tung, Rosemary Jones : 'A Portrait of Lost Tibet'; 1980 : 159-60.
4. *Ibid.*
5. Gergan, S.S. : 'The Lo-sar of Ladakh, Spiti, Lahul, Khinnu and Western Tibet', *The Tibet Journal*; Vol. 3, No. 3, Autumn – 78, 1978 : 41-43.
6. *Ibid.*

7. *Ibid.*
8. *Ibid.*
9. *Ibid.*
10. mashal : Me-to.
11. Galdan lang chot : Namgang (Tib. dg'a ldan lngam mchod).
12. Ladakhi belief that King Jamyang Namgyal of the 15th century issued a countrywide call for battle against the Cho of Skardo. It was unanimously later decided that 'Lo-sar' be celebrated in advance with a view of encountering a better fate in the battlefield and also, should there be no survivors to return for the celebration. The battle was in fact won and thus, Lo-sar is traditionally celebrated in the eleventh month. Thus the date of the said festival changed from early spring to winter in order to have better luck for the invasion of Balti Cho. Cf. Gergan, S.S.; *op.cit.*
13. Ka = Beam.
14. Zot = Store Room.
15. Chotkhang = Temple Room.
16. Tangra = Animals stay.
17. Tarcoks : Religious flags.
18. Chag zen : Tib. phyag-zan.
19. Abi-Meme : Old man and woman.
20. Srang-thug : Tib. srang-thug.
21. Co-Bumskyang : People in Nubra belief (Tib. Co-Bum-rkang) that once there was a devil in Nubra, in his food he required a child of less than eight years old. One day he called all villagers and said : "Do you see that hillock ? Go and cut it into pieces, I need plain so that I could see sun rise." It was a difficult task. Villagers sat together at one place and were discussing, how could they solve this problem. Among them one old lady was very close to Devil's wife. They requested the lady : "To go to the Devil's wife and ask the weakness of Co-Bumskyang."

    The lady did the same and asked : "Kindly let me know the weakness of Co-Bumskyang."

    "Co-Bumskyang is very brave you can't kill him, but he doesn't go near fire, therefore can be threaten by fire."

    This lady carried this information to villagers, who instead of working at hillock went near Co-Bumskyang's place, started diging a big trench. Thereafter they made *mashals* and threw them like missiles. Finally a mashal hit him and he fell near trunch. Villagers then killed him by throwing several mashals and stones. In this way in the new year villagers lead their life happily.

In Tibet at the end of the year at the monasteries, lamas celebrate annual festivals by performing chams. At the end they throw Tor-ma. It is said by doing this all the evil spirits who are hiding here and there leave the place, do not harm anyone. In the new year on the first, ninth, nineteenth and twentyninth they offer prayer to cooldown the activity of ferocious spirits. They make a symbol of ling-ga, later throw it away by litting fire.

In some parts of Tibet people mixed sugar, paper piece, silver polished piece of wood, piece of coal, yak hair, pieces of harbs etc. with flour, offer the same to their friends and relatives during day. Each family member is asked to pick up one piece. A person who gets piece of paper represents the quality of scholar; if he gets wooden piece indicates poorness; on piece of dung means of having good future, and by having pieces of harbs, he is supposed to win over his enemies. In the Central Tibet people see each corner of their rooms by mashals, later come by crying 'kye-ho....kye-ho....kye-ho", bylistening this voice other family members also come out speedily, throw their mashals outside of their villages and set firecrackers.

22. skying = skin, which looks as Ibex.
23. Kitchen almirah = langs.
24. On this occasion in Kinnaur the married women wear nyoza garland, visit th their houses, say 'Los-Cuma-tasis' or happy Lo-sar. In Ldakh also, brother and sistersgo to their houses, meet their mother and father, say Lo-sar la zal skyid nga sis de legsor happy Lo-sar.

    On this day they offer chhang by chabskyang after putting a piece of butter at its top called 'yar'. This time they say: Aba Ju, Ama Ju, Meme Jut etc. In Choshod village married women carried Pungpa or Karu (a big pot). This pots are full of chhang, after putting 'yar' on the mouth of their Pungpas as well as the bowls of their relatives, they offer chhang and say:

    Thap Ju, Thapla gyamo Ju
    Aaba Ju, Thapla gyamo Ju

Aama Ju, Thapla gyamo Ju
Aacho Ju, Thapla gyamo Ju,
Aacho Ju, Thapla gyamo Ju

In this way they pay regards to all their elders and offer chhang.

25. Mon and Gara : Those who have lower status in the Buddhist society.
26. Torma : Bela (to throw bala or evil spirits out).
27. Sattu : Fried flour.
28. Bad year left behind, welcome to new year.
29. Phasphuns: A group of families who has one 'lha' or Ishta-Deva and whose members help each other in the event of birth or death.
30. Sta-gyus : Horse race.
31. Lardak : Probably the main singer who sing folk songs during important occasions.
32. Lama Jugu : Two men after wearings masks perform dance during Lo-sar.
33. Khadags : op. cit.
34. Kangs : White scraf.
35. Hop pala hop seri phong : In the Lo-sar festival people after throwing Me-to return home say this slogan.
36. Daman : Musical instrument.
37. Losar – Tashis delaks – Jully.
38. Te-thap : This is a kind of drama performed during Lo-sar.
39. Kharpon: Who look after Khar (or palace).
40. Kompa Sumsek : It is a three steps dance, in all the important social ceremonies people in circle perform this dance.
41. Chot-khang : Family temple which is mostly built on the roof of family house building.
42. Aa-ba ; father.
43. Aa – ma : Mother.
44. Thukpa : It is a soup which is made by dry paneer, peas, green vegetables etc.
45. Tashi daleks : Welcome in Ladakhi dance and very much popular in Chang-thang region of Ladakh.
46. Jabro - It is Ladakhi Dance and very much popular in Chang-Thang region of Ladakh.
47. Chhang : A drink like beer.

7

Matho Monastery

A couple of days back, perhaps in the first week of April 2006, I came in contact with Lama Namgyal, a student of Central Institute of Buddhist Studies, Choglamsar, Leh-Ladakh, belongs to the Matho monastery. I was planning to write on Matho monastery, this was a healthy occasion for me to inquire more about the same. Soon after, he requested me to come to Lama hostel. I accepted the request. In his room I saw some books and papers written in Bodhi. Inquiring about them Namgyal said : "Some of them belong to Sakya tradition and history of Matho monastery."

"Yeah, That's I needed, could you please translate these for me?"

"Why not, but it would be nice if you accompany me for Matho."

"It's my pleasure."

"7th April 2006, is it O.K. ?"

"Oh. Yes!"

On 7th April evening, Lama Namgyal was searching me, he came to my class. I was not at my room, went to his hostel and waiting him there. About 4.30 he came, "Guruji ! You are here, I was searching you in college campus, any way tell me your programme."

"I'am ready, let's go."

"O.K."

He put my file in his bag. We walked down to Choglamsar bridge, popularly called 'Zampa', a stone throw distance from institute campus. About 5 P.M. Matho minibus arrived. It was overcrowded, but with the kind support of Lama Namgyal I was given seat. In Ladakh lamas have great respect, people without knowing them pay their regards. In this bus too they offered seat to lama Namgyal. This time I was obliged. Matho is 16 km from Choglamsar and 24 km from Leh, about half an hour we reached there. Namgyal's house was about 1 km from the Matho bus stand. We slowly walked upto his house. Namgyal's mother was awaiting us at the gate. She welcomed me by saying "Julley." "Julley Aa ma le" I replied I saw some cattle viz. sheep, goat etc. outside of his house. "Why do you keep them like this ?" "During day we keep them in open pen, at night take them to safer place."

In Ladakh pens are called 'nyi ra'. I surprise to see some white leghorn hens reared along with cattle. In 1998, I saw such practice at Takshi Parchathang in Nubra subdivision of Leh district. Generally poultry rearing is common among Muslims in Ladakh. This time if Buddhists also follow the same practice, it is a healthy sign for subsidiary industry in agriculture sector.

Lama Namgyal and his mother invited me at Guest room called *Don-khang (Tib. mgron khang)*. It had four small Ladakhi tables or cog-se *(Tib. cog-tse)*, decorated by Dregons *(Tib.grug)*. Dregons, infact not found in Ladakh, but paintings of such animals on *cog-tse*, represent auspicious symbol. Therefore, put in front the honourable guest.

After sometime Namgyal's sister Tsering Lhamo gracefully greeted me. She is my student, offered tea (Tib. za-mngar-mo) and bread slices. As soon I finished tea, she brought Ladakhi tea 'Solja' (Tib. gsol –za) and offered it in one cup. It was made of by butter, Tse-thang,milk and salt. Ladakhis at first take some water and boil it with Ladakhi tea, later pour it into Gur-Gur pot (i.e. srubs-ma), mix butter, milk and salt by piston.

A small wild animal effigy hanged through a wall facing to east near window. "What do you call this animal ?" I inquired.

"Kogar *(Tib. go-gar).* " Namgyal replied.

"How did you catch this ?"

"Once Kogar came to our animals pen, hens were also there. It was night, hens flew here and there, my father went into the pen. Kogar was hiding at the corner of wall, thus easily killed by stick."

I saw Kogar (Felis manul) at Choglamsar village, near the bank of Indus river. A full grown male measured one foot and one inch with long tail 8.5 inches. The body hair gave curious silvery appearance of shades of brown marked with blackish brown. On its back I saw deep brown strips, lower portion was pure white. The limbs in parts were tawny marked with black and head was marked with irregular sports. It had beautiful dense silky and long fur.

After some time Namgyal's mother brought a glass of milk.

"Aa ma le ! Why did you bring milk for me ?"

"Please, have it."

"I already have had bread, tea etc."

I took Ladakhi biscuits with milk. These are called Puli (Tib. Pu-li)' in Skrubuchan pronounced it as 'Pō lō', and in Nubra 'Pa'. The taste of these were like Kashmiri Kultcha. In the pot of Ladakhi biscuits, I saw one biscuit had a small piece of butter. I, inquired about the cause of it.

"It is called '*Yar*', signifies an auspicious symbol, whenever any ceremony occurs viz. during Pakston, Dun, Dagang etc. while serving chhang first time to guests 'yar' put on their respective cups."

Outside was cold, but quite warm inside, one *Bukhari* was burning in the room, time to time Namgyal's mother put *rikpa*, the dry dung as fuel. Soon after by 7 o'clock electricity came, all rooms lighted. Here electricity is supplied by diesel generator. Lama Namgyal has T.V. and D.T.H. connection.

"National programme doesn't come in T.V." I inquired. "It comes, may be any screw loose."

"Lama Namgyal was watching T.V. patiently. I thought to break the ice."

'What was your name before entering the Sangha?"

"Tsering Namgyal, when I took admission in Sangha of Matho monastery, head lama of the monastery gave me new name Jamyang Namgyal. During 1968, Luding Khen Rinpoche Jamyang Nyima was the head of Matho, therefore, according to his name all the lamas who were given admission in the monastery named after him as Jamyang Namgyal, Jamyang Tsephel, Jamyang Tamchos etc. Similarly by Stanpa': Stanpa Jamyang, Stanpa Wangchok etc. and from Nyima to Nyima Chosphel, Nyima Tsering etc. Earlier it didn't have head lama for some years."

"Every Buddhist has Puja room called 'Chot-khang'. To see Namgyal's 'Chot-khang', I climed stairs. In this room I saw two Buddha statues and a few thankas of Padmasambhava, Sakya Pandita and Buddha; framed photos of Heyvejra, Manjusri, Green tara and three head lamas of Sakya sect, e.g. Sakya Trizin Rinpoche, Ngor Luding Khen Rinpoche and Tsar Thrichen Rinpoche; they belong to the three subsects of Sakya tradition. The Matho monastery belongs to Ngor subsect of Sakya tradition.

Returing from Chot-khang I went to Namgyal's kitchen. In Ladakhi it is called '*chan-sa*'. There were many utensils, properly placed in a almirah, fixed at the north side wall,the other two sides had small Ladakhi tables and woollen carpets for guests. In olden days Ladakhis had big '*chan-se*', so that during important ceremonies, e.g. *Pakston, Dun, Dagang* etc. guests may be easily accommodated. Nowadays '*chan-sa*' is a small room like others. However, in important ceremonies they use tents.

On 10 o'clock Namgyal's mother served dinner. I took rice and dal, and went to bed. However, before going to sleep I was given bed tea.

Next day morning about 7 o'clock *Aa-ma-le* served tea and Ladakhi black tea (i.e. *ca-kunak*). It was cloudy morning, cold breeze was blowing.I didn't forget my plan after taking breakfast at 7.30 got ready for Matho monastery, and by 8 o'clock reached there. Lama Namgyal went to *comner (i.e. Pujari)* and brought Dukhang Nyingpa (temple) key.

This Dukhang was constructed by Lama Dungpa Dorje (i.e. Lama Dungpa Palsang Dorje). It has following Buddhist statues :

1. Avalokitesvara : 1000 hands and eyes
   : Standing posture
   : About 5 feet in height with eleven faces. This is the center statue.
2. Buddha Sakyamuni : Right to the center statue
   : Height – 4.5 feet
   : Bhumisparsa mudra
   : Sariputra and Maudgalyayana are standing on its right and left sides.
3. Verocana : Left to the center statue
   : Meditation mudra
   : height 4 feet
4. Rigsum gonpo peaceful form : They are three in number

(i) Avalokitesvara, height 5.5 feet. It is the center statue

(ii) Left to the center, 3 feet in height, Vajrapani

(iii) Right of the center, 3 feet in height, Jamyang

Besides it has the following wall paintings :
Outside wall along the door :
Left side : (1) Virupaksha
(2) Vaisravana
Right side : (3) Dhritarashtra
(4) Virudhaka
Inside Dukhang : Right side of the Central Statue

(1) Janyang mar ser ; manjusri in Red and yellow mixed colour

(2) Lama Zusdak Tsulthim Rinchen :
- He is the center image
- Weared red cap and robe
- Holds pen his right hand and paper in left
- Offered Jewels, Dharma Cakra and fruits

He is surrounded by the following Buddhist saints :
(i) Biropa
(ii) Mila
(iii) Unidentified
(iv) Chosgyal
(v) Paldan choskyong
(vi) Rinchen Migyur Gyaltsen
(vii) Rinchen Choszot
(viii) Paldan Choskyong
(ix) Unidentified
(x) Panchen Nagvang Kungga Ishes Wangchuk
(xi) Jamyang Khenese
(xii) Kunga Lotos

(3) Norchen Kunga Zangpo
- Centre figure and the founder of Norpa sub sect of Shakya tradition.
- Holds Vajra with flower in right hand and bell with flower in left.
- Seated in Dharmacakra mudra

- Weared red cap, upper and lower robe are slightly yellowish.
- A standing lama offer *nobu* and plant with white scarf on his left.
- Another lama is offering *norbu* with plant and blue scarf.
- Infront of him on the table from left to right; pot of wheat (nas), white damaru, mirror, skull and *pungpa* are offered.

In the mandala of Norchen Kunga Zangpo from right upper to down side the following figures can be seen :

(i) Kunga
(ii) Kunga gyaltsen
(iii) Dudul Wangcuk
(iv) Kunga Rinchan

(4) Verocana : center image
: white in colour
: Dhyana mudra
: Seated with four heads

In the mandala he has the following deities :

(i) sakya rivang sero
(ii) Lchakdog
(iii) Jogkar rung Zamar
(iv) Dorje snon po sngon po
(v) Dorje Gyu Sero
(vi) Dorje Marpo
(vii) Gaskaro
(viii) Marme ma
(ix) Luma Karo
(x) Marcher Lgangkhu
(xi) Dorje las snatasogs
(xii) Ti chabma ljang khu
(xiii) Dolma zangku (Green Tara)
(xiv) Srung Wasero
(xv) Tilbu maljang khu
(xvi) Karma ljang khu
(xvii) Dorje nod jin nakpo

(xviii) Dorje khu tsur serpo
(xix) Unidentified
(xx) Nyadpa Karpo
(xxi) Namkha Dog chan
(xxii) Rzizat mar ser
(xxiii) Metok ma sermo
(xxiv) Rinchen Serpo
(xxv) Mama ki snong
(xxvi) Threng sermo
(xxvii) Ljags pa sero
(xxviii) Lagpa ljang
(xxix) Ring chen sngong po
(xxx) Dhug sposma
(xxxi) Chag pa marpo
(xxxii) Chanma Karmo
(xxxiii) Gegmo karpo
(xxxiv) Gyalpo serpo
(xxxv) Darsem karpo
(xxxvi) Lchak kyu karpo
(xxxvii) Jung Gyal

Besides near the gate on the right side I saw the following Buddhist Deities

(i) Jung po dul jet
(ii) Tandin (Hdyegriva)

(5) Chepakmet : Centre figure

- colour : Red
- Mudra : Meditation
- Holds *pungpa*
- Wears upper green scarf, lower robe blue and red.

In the mandala the following deities are depicted :-

(i) Sakya Lama
(ii) Hdyegriva
(iii) Vajrapani
(iv) Khyung

(v) Rie Tsun mi yo wa
(vi) Namgyal ma
(vii) Jamyang
(viii) Kuru kule
(ix) Tsog sdhak lang na
(x) Yam chen mo

(6) Gonpo Dandi : center figure
- Seated, two hands
- Colour: black mixed blue

The following deities are depicted in the mandala
(i) Bata Nagpo
(ii) Dhod Kham Wangchuk ma
(iii) Nagmo Nodjin Yum
(iv) Puta
(v) 'akajati
(vi) Mag Zorma
(vii) Nagpo Nodjin yap
(viii) Sring moral chigma

In the middle of Puta and Sring maral chig ma one old black lady is depicted who carries dorje in her right hand and skull cup in her left.

The following deities are shown just below the center figure of Gonpo Dandi:
(i) Geylong
(ii) Pudmet
(iii) Skyes pa (a symbol of soldier)
(iv) Zanak

On the right of Gonpo Dandi the following deities are depicted
(i) lasgon
(ii) dram zuk
(iii) zal zipa dram zi zug chan
(iv) Jigjet
(v) Tur dak
(vi) Chagdor

On the wall above the door the following deities are depicted from left to right –

(i) Vajra pani
(ii) Avalokitersvara
(iii) Manjusri

All are in standing posture

(7) Vajraguru (or Padmasambhava)
- Behind the Bum pothi
- Weared red cap
- Holds skull pot, trishul, norbu and plant at the gap of left hand. This hand in meditation mudra
- Right hand placed near heart
- Weaved red *tsamtse*, orange chosgos, blue robe, green belt
- Seated (probably in meditation mudra)
- On his left and right two ladies from *Nag Lok* in standing posture

(8) Sachen Kunga Nying Po:
- Centre figure
- Depicted on the left wall of the Dukhang
- Meditation mudra
- Right hand holds flower, left hand in varadata mudra
- Without cap, yellow robe with red belt, covered by blue robe, brown chorgos

In mandala the following deities are depicted

(i) Lopon sodnam rtse mo
(ii) Rtsewn rinpoche dag pas gyaltsen
(iii) Palnamo
(iv) Sakya Pandita
(v) Sakya lama
(vi) Chosgyal phagspa
(vii) Sakya pandita

(9) Gyalva lozang drag pe : Centre figure
- dharmacakra mudra
- holds sword with flower in his right hand pothi with flower in his left
- Asana : Meditation

The following deities are depicted in his mandala-

(i) Gyalsabje (centre) Tsongkhapa
- Gyalsabje (Right side)
- khaduje (Left ride)
- Both are in Dharmacakra mudra

(ii) Geluk pa lama : Upper side of Tsongkhapa
: Below Atisa in Dharmacakra mudra; weared red cap, choagos and santap.

(iii) Gye dhun dup :
- Left to Tsongkhapa
- A Gelukpa Lama

(iv) Gelukpa Lama :
- Below Khaduje
- Yellow cap, red chosgos and yellow *Tsamtse*

(iv) Jamgon tashis :
- Upper side at the side of gye dhun dup
- Bhumisparsha mudra

(10) Sakya Pandita : Centre figure
- Dharmacakra mudra
- Weared red cap, chosgos and Tsamtse.

In his mandala the deities are :

(i) Sangyas Phunchog :
- Dharmacakra mudra
- Holds vjra in his right hand and left in meditation mudra.

(ii) Jamyang Sangyas
- Dharmacakra mudra
- Weared red cap, red chosgos and red tsamtse.

(iii) Chamba Sodnam Zangpo :
- Meditation mudra
- weared red cap, red chosgos and yellow tsamtse.

(iv) Namkha sandup :
- Dharmacakra mudra
- Left hand with *mani* norbu in meditation mudra.

(11) Medician Buddha : Centre Figure
- Body colour blue.
- Left hand holds *lunze* right with plant in varada mudra

- Ngagawang namgyal at his left depicted in Bhumisparsha mudra.

(12) Arya Avalokitesvara : Centre figure.
- Four heads.
- Colour white.

In the mandala the deities are:

(i) White Tara (Dolkar)
- Right to Avalokitesvara.
- Right hand in Varadata mudra.

(ii) Singeda – Right to Avalokitesvara.
- holds *trishul* in his right hand
- Lion skin used as asana.

(iii) Jigrten gunpo – Left to center figure.
- Drigung pa lama.

(iv) Dolzang (Green Tara)
- colour green.

(v) Tsering ma – Lion vahana
- holds vajra in her right hand and pot in her left.

(13) Namsras terdhak gyat :
- center figure.
- Vahana : white lion.
- Colour : Golden colour.

In his mandala eight gods are in worrior forms depicted with their vahanas (i.e. horses).

(14) Tam Chan Chosgyal :
- Body like Gonpo
- Three eyes.
- Human skulls garland.
- Crown: Five skulls.

On the opposite wall to window at Namling of old Dukhang has many frescos as described below.

On the first row:

(i) Sakyamuni Buddha :

- Centre figure in bhumisparshara mudra.
- His two disciples Sari Putra and Maudgalyana are standing on his right and left sides.
- Eight Indian pandits (Tib. Gyantug Chogni) are depicted in the mandala of the center figure.

On the second row :

(i) Gong ma nam nga
- Centre figure.

(ii) Unidentified lama.

(ii) Unidentified lama.

After completing research work in old Dukhang by late evening I alongwith Lama Namgyal returned to his house. Nest day, again started research work in New Dukhang. Here follows the details :

Fescos in New Dukhang

Left side of the door

(i) Centre Figure : Dung pa dorje pal zang. The following deities are depicted in the mandala of the center figure
Dubs thabs rgbya rtsa nas jung we duker mo :
- Right side up of the center figure.

(ii) Rong tsan kar po :
- Riding on horse with wrathful form.
- Right side down of the centre figure.

(iii) Green Tara :
- Left side up of the center figure.
- Seated with fine golden crowns.

(iv) Rong tsan mar po :
- Riding on red horse in wrathful form.
- Left side down of the center figure.

(vi) Dorje Mithukpa :
Centre up of the Dang pa dorje pal zang.

2. Sakya Trizin Nag Wang Kunga thek chen pal bar trinles Wang gi gyalpo

- Centre figure.
- Wear red cap, red chosgos and golden tramtse.
- Body white in colour.

In the mandala of the center figure are :

(i) ngor ludhing khanpo jamyung stanpe nyia
- Right side down of the center figure.
- Body : White.
- Crown cap.

(ii) Chepakmet :
- Right side in the middle of the center figure.
- Body colour : Red.

(iii) Tsuktor nampar gyal ma :
- Right side down of the center figure.
- Three faces, middle white; right side golden and left blue.

(iv) Dayang Lhamoyang chan ma :
- Left side down of the center figure.
- Body colour : White.

(v) Dolkar :
- White Tara
- Left side up of the center figure.

3. Snyan gyut gyat tsoi nga dhag tsar chen dorje :
- Centre figure.
- Body colour : Golden.

The following figures are depicted in his mandala

(i) jampal yang ngos khyen tseiwang poi zhabs :
- Body ; white colour.
- Holds vajra and sword in varadata mudra; left hand holds bell in the middle of the Asana.

(ii) sang dhag ngos jon loter wang poi zhabs :
- Left of the center figure down side.
- Body colour; white mixed red.

(iii) khas dup je we tsug gyan naropa:
- Right of the center figure on upper side.

(iv) ludub gya tso sang chen nor bui zot :
- Body; white mixed red colour.
- Right hand varadata mudra and left in meditation mudra.

(v) dub pa chog gi dhed pon dam ze che :
- Left side up of the center figure.
- Body; Pink colour.
- Dress; White.

(vi) zab sang zod zin khyen tse wang chug zhabs:
- Body; White mixed pink
- Dress : Red colour.

4. Gyal was lung stan ngor chen zhe :
- Body; Golden.
- Dress; Cap and other cloths red.
- Both hands in Dharmacakra mudra.

The following figures are shown in the mandala :

(i) shar chen yeshes gyatsen zhabs :
- Body; White mixed with pink.
- Holds pothi by both hands in the middle of the Asana.
- Right up of the center figure.

(ii) mra we nyi ma goram zhe :
- Dress; red with red cap.
- Right hand in Dharmacakra mudra and pothi in the left hand.
- Right hand in middle of the center figure.

(iii) khan chen khas dub gyal tsoi zhabs :
- Right lower side of the center figure.
- Right hand in varadata mudra, left in meditation form holds *mani.*

(vi) dub pe wang po Buddha sri:
- Body: White with pink colour.
- Dress : Without cap other cloths are in red colour.
- Left up of the center figure.

(vii) jamyang konchog lung dup zhabs :
- Body; White with pink colour.
- Weared red cap and Bhikshu dress.
- Middle left of the center figure.

(vi) shar chen lung rtogs gyal tsan zabs :
- Left down side of the center figure.
- Conical golden cap other wear red monk dress.

5. rtse chen kungga snying poi zhabs :
- Body; golden.
- Red cap, inner white robe, white coat, lower golden colour tsamtse.
- Centre figure.

In this mandala the following figures are depicted :

(i) jalus ngos dup sodnam rtse :
- Dharmacakra mudra
- Right up of the center figure.

(ii) sakya panchen kungai tsan:
- Right down side of the center figure.
- Asana; meditation.

(iii) dub chog drag pa gyaltsen zhabs :
- Body; white with pink colour.
- Left up of the center figure.

(iv) phags pa lotos gyaltsen zabs:
- Left down side of the center figure.
- Wear red cap and red colour lama dress.

6. sri zhi schi padma sambhava :
- Centre figure.
- Body golden.

- Right hand holds vajra in the middle of the chest; left hand holds skull cup, trishul with human skull.

In his mandala the following frescos can be seen :

(i) gyalwas lung snags phags chog ludub zhabs :
- Right up of the center figure,
- Asana : Right leg close, left open.

(ii) lta ngan mu stegs tsar chat phags pa lha :
- Below the Sl. No. (i) in the right side of the center figure.
- Asana: Right leg open, left close.

(iii) phas rgol stobs joms chogs kyi lang po gyal :
- Wear red cap and lama dress.
- Below the Sl. No. (ii) figure at the right side of center.

(iv) bum thak dhul wai zot zin yon tan ot :
- Below the Sl. No. (iii) figure
- Debate mudra, right hand up, left hand and face facing towards earth.

(v) phag yul sing tai srol zet thog met tsan :
- Left up of the center figure.
- Red cap, inner green, other red lama dress.

(vi) chos ngon gya tsoi zot zin yig nyen zabs :
- Below the Sl. No. (v) figure.
- Mudra : Debate.

(vii) rtsod gyal rig pe wang chug chos kyi dags :
- Below the Sl. No. (vi) figure.
- Mudra :Debate.

(viii) sripaizag pa yongs zad skya odth
- Below the Sl. No. (vii) figure.
- Mudra: Debate.

7. Sakyamuni Buddha :
   - Center figure.
   - Body : Golden colour.
   - Mudra : Bhumisparsha

In his mandala the following Buddhist scholars are depicted :

(i) Miphampa :
   - Right up of the center figure.
   - Mudra: Dharmacakra.

(ii) de not leg dut kung gao :
   - Below the Sl. No. (i).
   - Without cap wear red colour lama dress.

(iii) leng stan dud dul nyer bas chog :
   - Below the Sl. No. (ii).
   - Without cap wear red colour lama dress.

(iv) nyin mor cet pa nay poi zabs :
   - Below the Sl. No. (iii).
   - Without cap wear red colour lama dress.

(v) gyal chabs chog gyur ot sung tse :
   - Left up of the center figure.
   - Asana: Dolma style.

(vi) nog cin dul zat sane cos chen ;
   - below the Sl. No. (v).
   - Asana : Right leg knee on the left leg.

(vii) ta ngan chus zat de ti ka :
   - Below the Sl. No. (vi).
   - Mudra : Left hand in Dharmacakra and right hand in Bhumisparsha.

(viii) nga gya tul wa legs thong che :
   - Below the Sl. No. (viii).
   - Debate Mudra.

8. bara da za ser can la :
   - Mudra : Meditation.
   - Dress : Red colour lama.

9. hags pe nas tan ser byu :
   - Mudra : holds second finger of the right hand.
   - Asana : Dolma style.

10. phags pe nas tan zang po ni :
    - Mudra: Dharmacakra, left hand in meditation.

11. Nastan dorje moi bu :
    - Left hand in varadata mudra.

12. phags pe nas tan dus dan nyi :
    - Left hand in varadata mudra.
    - Right hand near chest.

Below the phags pe nas tan dus dan nyi in the middle wall between the two windows phags pe ge nyen dham ta figure is depicted. He is not the Arhat.

13. phags pe nastan nags na nas :
    - Mudra : Right hand placed near Asana, left hand holds stick with flag.

14. phags pe nas tan mi phampa :
    - Mudra : Meditation.
    - Cover his head by robe.

15. phags pe nas tan yan lak zung :
    - Right hand holds stick with cloth near his heart.

16. sa tuk stok pa phul gyur nas sta ngan ri zik birupa :
    - Centre figure.
    - Mudra : Te chabs.

In his mandala the following Buddhist scholars are depicted :

(i) zag mo do de ton zig sin chod dal yak ston sangyas pal:
- Mudra : Dharmacakra.
- Right up of the center figure.

(ii) do ngag gons ton tal khas pa pan chen sakya chog dan jabs :
- Mudra : Dharmacakra.
- Below the Sl. No. (i).

(iii) dek sum chat la mi zik pe se za kun zik rongs tonze :
- Mudra : Ti chab
- Left up of the centre figure.

(iv) rab zam gyud de mar vang zong pa kung ga namgyal chog :
- Below the Sl. No. (iii).
- Mudra : Ti chab.

17. Kadam stan pe mig cet Atisa ;
- Up right side.
- Mudra : Dharmacakra.

18. zha ser stan pe srog shing lozang daks :
- Mudra : Dharmacakra.
- Below the Sl. No. (17).

19. dup pe gyal tsen denge khas mi la ze :
- Without cap white dress.
- Left upper side.

20. theg pa chog gi sing ta long chen chog
- Below the Sl. No. (19).
- Mudra : Bhumisparsha.

21. phags pe nas tan Bakula.

22. phags pe nas tan da can zin :
- Holds five crown caps.

23. phags pe nas tan lam than stan.
    - Meditation mudra.

24. Bara da za sod nyuoms len :
    - Right hand holds pothi.
    - Left hand holds lungze.

25. phags pe nas tan lam tan ni :
    - Right hand in Dharmachakra mudra, left hand holds pothi.

26. phags pe nas tan lu yi de :
    - Right hand holds pot.
    - Left hand holds kharsil.

27. phags pe nas tan sbet chet ni :
    - Both hands hold pothi in the middle of the Asana.

28. phags pe nas tan mi chet pa :
    - Holds stupa.

Below the kadam stan pe mig cet Atisa and phags pe nas tan Bakula; sangyas khor ces can dangs pe zor dan gyal po ha sang ze is depicted. Similarly below the Bara da za sod nyuoms len, not sjin ter dak gyal tsen nam tos sras is depicted.

Along the door

29. Kundrik nampar nagzat :
    - Body colour : White.
    - Face : Four.
    - Asana and Mudra : Meditation.

In his mandala the following deities are depicted :

(i) Lo chen rin chen zang po :
    Mudra and Asana : Meditation.
    - Right up of the center figure.

(ii) Tandin :
    - Wrathful form.

- Below the Sl. No. (i) figure

(iii) Kyung tha :
- Wrathful form.
- Below the Sl. No. (ii).

(iv) Singe da :
- Left up of the center figure.
- body : white colour.

(v) Sing dong ma :
- Below the Sl. No. (iv).
- Wrathful form.

(vi) Zam nak :
- Below the Sl. No. (v).
- Wrathful form.

30. Gonkar :
- Centre figure.
- Body: White colour.

In the mandala the deities are :

(i) Zam ser :
- Left up of the center figure.
- Asana: Dolma style.

(ii) Zam mar (yab yum):
- Below the Sl. No. (i).

(iii) Zam kar :
- Body: White colour.
- Right up of the center figure.

(iv) Zam lzang :
- Below the Sl. No. (iii).
- Yab-yum form.

On the wall above the door
Right to left

(i) Manjusri :
- Hands : Four.
- Body : Golden colour.
- Crown : Five golden.

(ii) Zung po dul cet :
- Wrathful form.
- Crown : Five skulls.
- Eye : Three.
- Body : Blue and black.

(iii) Avalokitesvara :
- Hands : Four.
- Mudra : Namaskar.
- Crown : Five golden.
- Body : White colour.

Statue in the New Dukhang
Sakyamuni Buddha :
- Centre statue.
- Height : 4'
- Width : 2'

Besides one throne is made for head lama. It is 9' 5" in height and 4'8" in width and made of wood with Ladakhi art.

Besides 108 small Buddha and one vajra pani statues are placed in the glass almirah.

There are 18 Buddhist texts in the glass almirah in whicl two pothis are old.

After completing research work in New Dukhang at 3 o'cloc I came down and waiting for local bus near a shop. At last about p.m. I got left in tipper, came to Chushod; thereafter by mini bı returned to Choglamsar. It was raining, weather was cold, therefor I took complete rest.

Next day in evening I went to Lama Namgyal room to clear my confusions.

"In olden days before Matho monastery, Matho Khar was constructed, is it true ?"

"At present left side below the monastery on a hillock we can see ruines of palace (Tib. Khar). As we know *rtse lhamo* belongs to all palaces in Ladakh. Here too *rtse lhamo* lives in this palace. It infers Matho Khar was built before Matho monastery. Furthermore we can see Kalon's Zurkhang near the ruined khar, it has fresco of Gur Goa, which is about five hundred years old. This also prove the above statement."

"Is it the same wall painting which was made by the nose blood of Lama Tungpa Dorje?"

"Yes sir, I think so, however, it would not possible to make painting from the blood only. Therefore, a small portion of the blood might be taken, mixed with other needed colours."

"When did lama Tungpa Dorje palzang arrive Ladakh? Whether he was invited by king Dragpa Bumde?"

"According to Ladakhi historians, Lama Tungpa Dorje himself visited Ladakh, later went for meditation near Matho village. As soon as King Dragspa Bumde came to know, he invited him for the construction of Tisaru (Tiseru) stupa near Leh. Tungpa Dorje visited the site, performed rituals called *rabnas*. Later stupa was constructed."

"Tiseru stupa was constructed during King Dragspa Bumlde."

"Yeah, as lama Tungpa Dorje completed all rituals like *Bhumi pujan* or rabnas for Tiseru stupa. King offered Matho, Stakna, Shey, Marshinlang etc. villages to him, asked to build Sakya order monasteries in these areas. Lama Tungpa Dorje thanked him and, came in Matho village. He stayed in Zurkhang. Thereafter, made fresco of Gur gon, which is still exist in Chotkhang of Zurkhang. Later he climed to a cave near the present Matho monastery for meditation. One day when he came out from the above cave saw two deers at the present monastery, who were sitting without any fear. He thought the presence of deers indicate the purity of the place. Therefore, he should construct monastery. Henceforth, he built a temple, which is known Gonkhang. In this way he founded Sakya tradition in Ladakh."

"Is present head lama of the Matho monastery incarnation of Tungpa Dorje?"

"After the parinirvana of Lama Tungpa Dorje, his incarnation was not found. Therefore, head lama of the Sakya order in Tibet authorized to nominate lama for Matho monastery as head lama in Ladakh."

"Thiksey and Spitug (Spituk) monasteries were also established during king Dragspa Bamde period, they have many branch gonpas, Matho does not have, what's the reason?"

"During Balti war, King Jamyang Namgyal recruited lamas from the Matho monastery as soldiers, unfortunately he lost the battle, many lamas lost their life. Baltis reached upto Matho and destroyed monastery badly. King got imprisonment and was taken to Skardu. As a result Marshilang and Stakna separated from the Matho. However, king was released under some conditions. This news spread throughout in Tibet. Lama Choskyi Lotos from Tibet came in Ladakh and met king Jamyang Namgyal. He informed him how Matho monastery was destroyed by Baltis. King promised to renovate the monastery and would provide all necessary help. But king suddenly died. This verbal promises between King Jamyang Namgyal and Lama Choskyi Lotos not being conveyed to his ministers. When Singge Namgyal became king, Stag Stang Raspa became the king's priest, thus according to his tradition king promoted Drugpa K'agyud monasteries in Ladakh. The Shey,

Stakna and Marshilang which were earlier under the Sakya changed into Drugpa order."

"I saw tangra just below the monastery, what is the use of this?"

"During Nagrang, Lhas go to *Phu* to change Lhato on 8th of the second month of the Tibetan calendar. Their horses which are brought here before Nagrang, kept here till they return from Phu. It is called Chibra."

"I saw here many Lhatos, what do you say about them?"

"In Matho we have different groups of Phasphuns, these Lhatos are made according to their faith."

"Near the monastery we can see five heads chortens, are these have some relation with Rignga?"

"Yes, the five heads of the chortens represent to Rig nga i.e. the five Dhyani Buddhas. They are eight in number. Four protects the village, other protects monastery from evil spirits.

In olden days to listen Ka-wang, lamas from Ladakh sent to Tibet. However, lamas of Nor-pa Sakya tradition were free for Ka-wang offer. The head lama of Matho monastery therefore, changed the Monastic system into Norba. Thereafter to increase the strength of lamas in the monastery the present eight five heads chortens were constructed. The present head lama of Matho monastery belongs to Nor-pa tradition since 1968. However, we don't know why such four chortens were constructed in Matho village after Choskyi Lotos?"

In the first week of August, I got the chance to visit Marshilang. In fact Angmo's mother died. Angmo is peon in Central Institute of Buddhist Studies, Choglamsar. Therefore, administrative authority of the institute had arranged bus for us. Normally, institute does not want to provide any kind of help to teachers who don't have any power except to teach students, fortunately this time the authority felt pity on us.

Oh! No, forget about the institute. I purchased a biscuit packet and sat at the corner of the bus. At Karu bridge, bus driver asked all teachers to to get down and go own foot. Poor teacher got down and climbed to Angmo's house on foot, in the institute car principal, administrative officer and office staff reached before us. However, we reached there just before the closing funeral ceremony. We were asked to take tea and some breads. After a few minutes started to return to Karu bridge. It was raining, principal felt pity on us, he asked car driver to pick up teachers. Any how we came to Karu. Office staff returned to institute by office car, we later by bus came to institute. Thus, in this poor country teachers or scholars have no value. The Government is run by high class clerks and institutes by similar ranks. Think, how India can get progress? Therefore, for the development of any country the concern authority will have to provide full facilities to scholar teachers. Well we understand that those who have sound knowledge want to live in a simple way, whereas those who don't have perfect knowledge carry the load of ignorance. Any how my visit to Marshilang was informative. It has one small gonpa, a Junior High School, a micro hydel project and five heads chorten near the settlement. I don't know whether it has any relation with Matho chortens or not, researchers may come forward and solve this question.

My study on Matho monastery was not yet completed. I once again requested Lama Namgyal to accompany me up to Matho. He accepted my request. We took bus from Choglamsar on 15th August morning. About half an hour at 10 a.m. reached monastery. Lama Namgyal went to *Pujari* for key. I waited him outside the Dukhang. *Pujari* was not in his room. To search him he went down stairs. About 11 o'clock he returned with key of the 'lhum grub khang' some time called Meseum of the monastery. I followed Lama Namgyal. In this temple I saw some beautiful murals, as stated below :

1. Kunzang khorlo.
2. Tokpo stakthit :
   (i) Plant

(ii) Sokpo with chhang pot.
(iii) Tiger.

3. Kalcakra Mantra called Namcu Wangdan.
4. to (11) : Eight offering deities, standing on one leg, right leg folds and stands on left. These have the following colours.
5. White flower ornament.
6. Orange.
7. Red.
8. Light green.
9. Golden.
10. White, holds flower with conch.
11. Blue.
12. Blue, without flower.

All the above deities are depicted standing posture on moon disce.

In the middle of the above deities the following things are painted according to five senses.

(i) Mirror with yellow colour vajra.
(ii) Violen.
(iii) White conch.
(iv) White zalze.
(v) Red cloth.

On the upper side the following things are depicted for chelanamsum prayer.

(i) Yellow chodpe.
(ii) Yellow pot with orange offering things.
(iii) Couch with red scarf.
(iv) Yellow fruit with green plant.
(v) Three white flutes tied with red scarf.
(vi) Lungje.
(vii) Yellow pot with orange thodpe.
(viii) White mirror with scarf.
(ix) Yellow wheel on moon disce with flower.

Below the eight flower offering deities, seven kinds of auspicious things are painted, as shown below from left to right.

(i) Yellow wheel.
(ii) Auspicious Mani.
(iii) Cun mo rinpoche.
(iv) Lonpo Rinpoche.
(v) Lanpo Rinpoche.
(vi) Stak chok Rinpoche.
(vii) Magpon Rinpoche.

If we study the concern religious pothi, the above religious items can be put in the following sequence.

1. Mirror.
2. Ghihang
3. Lingze
4. Durbil
5. Tung
6. Lithi
7. Yangkhar

One item fruit is not included.

13. On the wall between the two doors various kinds of Mani (jewel) and auspicious offerings are depicted.

14. The main figure on the wall is Amitayus with pot. On his right a yogi is shown in meditation posture. On his left various pictures is shown as :

(i) Flower plant.
(ii) Dolma with Dolma Photang.
(iii) At the right side of Photan sun and left side moon are painted.
(iv) Buddha, some animals (i.e. four friends) and Tsering tukor are depicted.

15. Kang Rinpoche with various monasteries, Manasarovar lake and three kinds chos are shown.

(i) Gonjong cho
(ii) Purang cho
(iii) Lhasa cho in a palace.

Paintings on the walls of Namling in lhun grub khang was partially damaged by rain. Renovation works have been undertaken in order to protect the rest paintings from rain and moisture. Here follows the details.

Paintings on the wall in front of the door

(i) Zungpo dulchet.

(ii) Three kinds lamas.

Paintings on the north-side wall

(iii) Buddha: Centre figure.

(iv) Sari Putra on the right and left sides of the center figure.

(v) Maudgalyayana

(vi) Birupa : Right of center figure.

(vii) Manjusri : 4 hands
: On the left and right sides head lamas of Sakya order.

(viii) Right corner : White Tara in standing posture.

(ix) Left corner : Green Tara in seated posture.

Wall paintings on the wall towards door

(x) Sakya Pandita

(xi) Guru Rinpoche

(xii) Sakya head lama

(xiii) Dharma protector in wrathful form.

Besides, there are some scroll paintings hanging with the walls in Namgling. The details is cited below.

1. Yamantaka – Centre.
2. Head lama of Sakya order – Right of center Thanka in the mandala various Sakya traditional deities are depicted.
3. Avalokitesvara:

Four hands with mandala. I saw some small Buddhist statue made of clay. The details is shown below.

(i) Tungshak Buddhas i.e. thirty five Buddhas.

(ii) Three Avalokitesvara: Four hands, seated.
(iii) Namgyal chorten.

Here some masks of various deities are hanged along the walls of Namling. The details is cited below.

(i) Kale Kava
(ii) Gonpo
(iii) Phumet
(iv) Turdok – two in number
(v) Yamantaka
(vi) Che-chang
(vii) Unidentified two black masks
(viii) Skeyespa – two in number

Along one side wall of this temple I saw some old precious religious things, preserved in the glass covered box. Here follows some of them:

1. Old weapons of·deities
2. Bell covers
3. Tung
4. Vajra Kila
5. Sword covers
6. Tranbed
7. Mask – two in number
8. Painting wooden blocks
9. Tiger skin for Nngrang oracles
10. Shoes of oracles
11. Head of oracles
12. Pungpa cover
13. Cover of tung
14. Yak effigy
15. Janak hat.

In the lhan grub khang I saw the following statues :

1. Maitrey
   Colour – white
   Posture – seated
   Height – 5'

2. Head Lama of Sakya order : He was the founder of Norpa sub-sect named Norchen Dorje Chang Kunga Zanpo

   Mudra - Dharmacakra
   Cap - Red hat
   Face - Golden colour
   Body - Golden colour
   Chosgos - Orange colour
   Height - 4'3"
   Width - 3'

4. Head Lama of Sakya order
   - At upper cupboard
   - Right hand in Dharmacakra mudra
   - Left hand in Meditation

   Cap - Red hat
   Chosgos - Orange
   Posture - Seated on throne
   Height - 27" with throne
   Width - 1' 5" along the throne.

5. Dogon Chosgyal Phagspa : Left of Head Lama of Sakya

   Cap - Red hat
   Chosgos – Red
   Body - Yellow
   Posture – Seated on Padma throne
   Mudra - Holds thumb and first finger of both hands and put them near the middle of chest
   Height – 10" with throne

5. Padmasambhava Height – 4"

6. Unidentified statue –Small statue - Ahead of the throne

7. Padmasambhava – Just below the almirah

   Height – 3'4"
   Posture – seated on throne
   Width – 2'8" with throne

8. Maitreya ; Behind Padmasambhava
Posture – Standing
Height – 2'6" with throne

One Hum mantra carved stone is placed just before the Maitrey statue.

Buddha : In the upper cupboard with his two disciples Sariputra and Maudgalayana
Posture - Seated with lungze pot in meditation mudra, Right hand Bhumisparsha and left in meditation mudra.

Dogon Chosgyal Phagspa : Placed in front of the Buddha
Height – 5"

Maitreya : Placed just below the head lama of Sakya lama
Posture : Seated
Height : 3'4" with throne of Padma
Mudra : Dharmacakra

Vajrapani : Upper side

Avalokitesvara : Upper side in the middle

Manjusri : other side of Avalokitesvara

Dolmas : Two in number.

Avalokitesvara: Height- 6"

Unidentified : Height-5"
: Posture-Standing.

Amitayus : Just below the above cupboard
Holds-Pot of longevity.
Mudra – Meditation.

Height – 4'3" with throne.
Width- 2'10"

20. Avalokitesvara : Back of Amitayus with tiger skin
Posture-standing.
Height-4'3"
Holds-Beats in right hand
Mudra-Two hands in Namaskar.

21. Avalokitesvara : Four hands
: In upper Cupboard
: Height-2'5"

22. Head Lama of Sakya order :
: Height –2"
: Cap-Red hat
: Chosgos-Red
: Body-Golden
: Clothes-Red.

23. One Lama : Small Statue
: Placed ahead of Head lama of Sakya order.

24. Tara : Small Statue
: next to lama.

25. Buddha : Standing posture.

26. Amitayas : Standing posture
Lama, Tara, Buddha and Amitayas placed left to right one after other.

27. Maitreya :
- Below Avalokitesvara Sl.No. 20.
- Height : 3'4"

28. Chanchub Chorten :
- Below Sl.No. 20.

- Height : 3'4"
- Right side of Maitreya.

28. Sachen Kung-ga Nyingpo:
    - In the upper cupboard, right side of the main statue.
    - Height : 5"

29. Lama :
    - Right of the Sl.No. 28 and Height : 4"

30. Lama : without hat
    - Right of the Sl. No. 29 and Height : 4"

31. Dorje Chang Kung-ga Zangpo :
    - Right of the Sl.No. 30 and Height 4"

32. Milarepa :
    - Right of Sl.No.31 and Height: 5"

Left side of the main statue Cupper cupboard Right to Left,

33. Birupa :
    Colour – Red
    Cloths - Yellow
    Throne – Golden flower
    Height – 4"
    Posture – Seated

34. Head lama of Sakya tradition:
    Cap – Red hat
    Cloths – Red
    Height – 2'7" with throne
    Width – 2'

35. Head lama of Sakya tradition :
    Cap – Red hat
    Clothes – Red

Stotgag – yellow
Body – yellow
Posture – Seated
Height – 3' with throne
Width – 2'7"
Location – Placed below Sl. No. 33.

36. Changchub chorten :
   - Upper cupboard behind the statue.

37. Buddha :
   Called Cho Rinpoche
   Holds : Pot in left hand
   Right hand : Bhumisparsha
   Height : 2'7"
   Width : 2'

38. Manjusri :
   - Ahead of Sl. No. 37 right to Buddha.
   - Height 4"

39. Manjusri :
   - Right to Sl.No. 38
   - Height : 4"

40. Six hands Mahakala:
   - Right to Sl.No.39
   - Height : 4"

41. Medicine Buddha :
   - Right to Sl.No.40.
   - Height : 5"

42. Chepakmet :
   - Below the upper cupboard
   - Without pot in meditation mudra
   - Height : 2'10"

- Width : 2'3"

42. Foot print :
    - Behind Chepakmet
    - It would be of Buddhist Siddha.

44. Avalokitesvara :
    - Upper Cupboard
    - Height : 4"

45. Avalokitesvara :
    - Right to Sl. No. 44.
    - Height : 4"

46. Avalokitesvara :
    - Right to Sl.No.45.
    - Height : 4"

47. Avalokitesvara :
    - Right to Sl. No. 46.
    - Height : 4"

48. Guru Rinpoche :
    - Right to Sl. No. 48.
    - Height : 4"

49. Manjusri :
    - Five crowns
    - Hand : Two
    - Height : 4' 4"
    - Width : 3'
    - Below the statue Sl.No. 48.

50. Unidentified :
    - Blue body
    - Posture: Seated like Birupa
    - Right side vajra kalika, five in number with wooden stand.

51. Vajrapani :
   - Wrathful form
   - Height : 2'10"
   - Width : 1'

52. Vajrapani :
   - Wrathful form
   - Height : 2'10"
   - Width : 1'

"In Ladakh during 15th century many Buddhist monasteries were established with the kind support of king Dragspa Bumde. Whether Matho monastery was also funded in the same century ? I asked.

"It seemed me, Gonkhang temple was funded during this period. However, 'lhun grub Khan' temple might be established later on probably in 18th century. " Lama Namgyal replied.

"Can you explain this historical point in more detail?"

"It said that due to some reason Ladakh King Phunchok Namgyal (1739-60) was not happy with the activities of Purig King Khuvo Tashis Namgyal. Later their relations became so controversial that would turn to war. This news reached to Tibet. Dalai Lama Stalzang Gyatso when came to know, he immediately called Kathok Tsewang Norbu from Nepal and sent him to Ladakh to solve the misunderstandings between Phunchok and Tashi Namgyal. Kathok Tsewang Norbu was earlier sent to Nepal to change the 'Shoksing' of 'Charung kha shor' Chorten. Kathok Tsewang Norbu talked both the kings of Ladakh and Parig alongwith their respective ministers at Vamle village. First meeting failed. Thereafter on his request series of meeting took in presence of Hemis Gyal sras Rinpoche, village heads called Gobas, respective lamas of gonpas, Representive of Lhasa, Kashmiri merchants etc.

Finally came to the following conclusion:

(i) Purig King Tashi Namgyal will look after the property of Purig citizens.

(ii) Puring King will not harass Kashmiri merchants and Purig citizens unnecessarily.

(iii) The eldest son of the king will become the next king of the Ladakh, other son will have to become lama. In one kingdom there is no possibility to have two kings. Therefore, all the younger sons of the king will have to follow the Vinayic rules and regulations of the concerned gonpa's head lamas.

He added the paintings of lhun grub khang was made during Kathok Tsewang Norbu period, he remarks.

On the wall along the door of 'lhun grub khang'. We can see Kungong khorlo (a grammer of Bodhi poetry), this indicates that wall paintings were in progress during the visit of Kathok Tsewang Norbu in Ladakh."

Hence, Matho gonpa was founded by king Dragspa Bomde during 15th century, later other temples constructed in the following years.

1. Gonkhang : 15th century.
2. lhun grub khang: It was earlier known kangyas Khang and was built during 18th century.
3. Dukhang Ningpa : Probably 18th century.
4. Dukhang Soma : 1970 by Matho Dharma Association.
5. Dolma Lhakhang
6. New kangyur khang

(5–6) Probably during 1971-75

My mind was once again attracted by five heads chartens. I was informed that such chartens were constructed during 10-11th century in Shey, Thiksey and Chemdey. But I didn't see these there. They may be in Thiksay Nyarma. I saw many ruin chortens there, which were built during 11th century. About the uniqueness of such chortens, Lama Namgyal explained:

"In Mahayana Buddhism, Tantra has four kinds ; Cha-gyud, cho-gyud, Nalzor-gyud and Nalzor-Lamet gyud Lotava Rinchen Zangpo practiced Nalzor Lamet gyud. The five heads chortens built under the tradition of Nalzor Lamet gyud. In Matho monastery such chortens were built very late during 16-17th century for the preservation and protection the monastery and for increasing the number of lama population in the monastery. These are the symbol of mandala. So, four of them built at the four directions and one near the main monastery building. In this way the monastery building may be preserved and protected from all kinds of evils who may harm the monastery."

Kangyur khang has two pillars, two windows and one big changchub chorten in the middle. This chorten is eight feet in high and 4'4" in width. One side wall of the temple has almirah in which Kangyur pothis are placed. At one side only one Buddha statue is placed. Besides I saw many Tibetan scroll paintings, hanged with the ceiling as described below.

1. Jigjed in peaceful form
2. Buddha Amitabha.
3. Unidentified.
4. Buddha with his two disciples - Sari Putra and Maudgalyaiyana
5. Vajradhra
6. Kurukule
7. Chogdak
8. Dhodgyal
9. Vajrasattva
10. Rigsum Gonpo
11. Buddha Amitabha
12. Lama Tagsan
13. Dolkar (white)
14. Opakmet
15. Avalokitesvara-four hands, seated.
16. Lontisa or Namtosras

(Items 5 to 7: These figures are framed and Sl.No. 6 to 8 are painted from left to right)

One small lhabad chorten made of sandal wood can be seen here.

Lham Das Khang temple of this monastery has some Buddhist statues made of clay, for details see below.

1. Dogan Chhogyal Phagspa : Centre Statue
2. Jamyang Shesrab Gyatso
3. Muschhen Sempspa chenpo
4. Nor chen rdo-rje' achang norchen dorje chang.
5. Khasdup Paldan Dorje
6. Gorampa Sonam Senge.
7. Lama Choskyi Lotos
8. Buddha
9. Tungha Dorje Palzang dung pa rdo-rje.
10. Yongzin Konchhog Phelwa.
11. Dorje chang.
12. Sachen Kunga Ningpo
13. –do-
14. –do-
15. Sakya Pandita
16. Dogon Chosgyal Phagspa
17. –do-
18. Zambala

(Items 12–18: all these status are 8" –10" in height and placed ahead of of the Gorampa sonam.)

19. One Sakya lama
20. Konchog Lhundup
21. Birupa
22. Jetsun Sangses Rinhyen Jetsun Gongma Namnga
    - (i) Sachen Kunga Nyingpo
    - (ii) Sadnam rlsemo
    - (iii) Jelsun Dalepa gyaltsen
    - (iv) Sakya Pandita Kungyaltsen
    - (v) Dogan Chosgyal Phugspa

S.No. (i) to (ii) are placed near the center statue, all these are small in height (i.e. 10" and width 9").

23. Gyalwa Lhachog Senge
24. Norchen Dorje ehang.
25. Dogon Chosgya Phgspa.
26. Gonpo
27. Gonpo

(Items 26–27: made of brass and small in height)

Lham Das Khang Lhakhang has one big been which is decorated by Budddhist Zhalar. Besides it is also decorated by thanka paintings.

The details is shown below :

1. Avalokitesvara : Four hands.

2. Buddha in Bhumisparsha mudra. There are two Buddhas also depicted in his mandala.

3. Buddha Sakyamuni with his two disciples-Sari putra and Maudgalyayana.

In the mandala the following deities are painted.

(i) Vajra Dhara : At the Centre.
(ii) Drogan Chosgyal Phagspa
(iii) Yogini khacotma
(iv) Heyvarjra (Keydor)
(v) Avalokitesvara-Four hands
(vi) Danje Jugcan
(vii) Turdag
(viii) Gonpo-two heads
(ix) Paldan Lhamo

4. Amitayus : In the mandala has

(i) Dolkar
(ii) Namgyalma
(iii) Sasen Kungga ningmpo
(iv) Sodnam Cemo
(v) Sakya Pandita
(vi) Jecum trakpa gyaltsen
(vii) Dogon Chosgyal Phagspa
(viii) Gonpo two hands
(ix) Jungpo Dulcet
(x) Bhumi Devi
(xi) Unidentified

5. Norchen Dorje Kunga Zangpo; Dharmachara mudra; holds plant with Dorje and bell.

6. White Tara with mandala.

7. Chepakmet: surrounded with lamas and various Buddhist deities.

8. Gyalva Lhachogs singge; surrounded by lamas.

9. Buddha Sakyamuni with sari putra and Maudgalyayana.

10. Avalokitesvara – 4 hands; surrounded by lamas of concerned Buddhist order.

11. Sachen Kungga Gyaltsen (or Sakya Pandita); surrounded by concerned sect.

12. Vajradhara; surrounded by lamas of sakya lamas.

13. Vajrasattva ; holds dorje in his both hands near the middle of chest.

14. Dogon chorgyal phagspa; surrounded by Buddha, white Tara and Budhisattvas.

15. Guru Padmsambhava (Guru Khanasum zilnon).

16. A thanka of Vajra Kalika, surrounded by Vajra Kalika.

17. White Mahakala; surrounded by Sakya lamas.

18. Guru Padmasambhava; surrounded by Avalokitesvara, Vajrapani, Amitayus and Bodhisatitvas.

19. Dolkar.

20. Head of Sakya lama, surrounded by Buddha, Gonpo and Bodhisattvs.

21. Guru Padmasambhava and Bodhisattvas.

22. Konkhon Gorampa Sodnam Singge Sunddan; surrounded by Buddha, Birupa, Saclen Kungga Ningpo and Boddhisattvas.

23. Unidentified : Towards the door along the wall first thanka
Height : 4' 3"
Width : 2'10"

24. Unidentified; yabyum : old; next to Sl.No. 23; with frame has the following measurements :
Height : 4' 2"
Width : 2'11"

25. White Tara (Tib. Dolkar) : surrounded by Vajradhara, Milarepa, Avalokitesvara and Vajrasttva; Height –4' 5" and width-3'

26. Manjusri; Two hands; surrounded by Dorje Chang, Sakya Pandita and Green Tara.

27. Buddha; surrounded by four Buddhas of four directions and chospe lhamo gyat in mandala.

28. Dancan chosgyat ; body in red colour.

29. Sakya lama, holds *mani* (Jewel) in left hand and Right hand in Dharmachakra mudra.

30. Yellow Tara; surrounded by Buddha and concerned Buddhist deities.

31. Avalokitesvara; standing posture, surrounded by Dharma protectors and Buddhist deities of the concerned sect.

32. Mahakala; Nagpo Thanka; two hands surrounded by wrathful Dharma protectors.

33. Avalokitesvara; 4 hands.

34. Vajrapani.

35. Unidentified.

36. Six hands Gonpo.

37. Two hands Gonpo.

38. Unidentified.

39. Vajrapani.

40. Unknown or Unidentified.

41. Unidentified.

42. Unidentified, A head lama of Sakya lama.

43. Unidentified mandala.

44. Mandala of Unidentified Buddhist deity.

45. Mandala of Buddha.

46. Mandala: of Unidentified Buddhist deity.

In lha Khang gyu lo khong I saw some Buddhist deities: Here follows the details.

1. Dolma : Main statue
   Height – 4' 5"
   Width –3'

2 to 21 : Twenty Dalma Statues each of height 2'3" and width 10"

Infront of the above statues has one mandal offer. At one corner of the temple four pairs or eight oracles hats are placed. Besides on glass framed photo of Gongma Nangnga and Norchen,

Charchen and Gonpo with two hands are placed along with 21 Dolma Thankas at the height of 3' and width 2'. Hanged with the ailing.

Lakung temple does not have statue. The details of wall paintings are shown below:

Lama Tungpa Dorje; the founder of Matho monastery sponsored wall paintings in this temple.

1. Kurgon : Two hands
   Height –5'
   Width-4' 4"

2. Sakya lama : Height-2' 11"
   Width –2' 4"

3. Buddha Amitabha :
   Height : 4' 11"
   Width : 4' 3"

4. A Lama painting destroyed by water or rain.
   Height –3'
   Width – 2' 8"

4. New paintings of Buddha in Namaskar mudra,
   Height – 3'
   Width – 2'8"

5. New Painting of Buddha in Namaskar mudra; Height –4' 8"
   Width- 4'3"

6. Sachen Kungga Ningpo
   Height-3' 7"
   Width- 3' 10"

7. Buddha :
   Left hand in meditation
   Right in Dharmachara mudra

Height : 4' 11"
Width : 3' 10"

8. A Head lama of Sakyapa order
Height 2' 10"
Width 2' 5"

9. Vajra Yogini:
Height –3' 6"
Width – 2' 5"

10. Unidentified like Dolma: Left hand holds bell. Right hand holds vajra near right side of her heart.

11. Vajradhara:
Body black, holds bell and dorje near the middle of his chest.

12. Buddha Sakyamuni with Sari Putra and Maudgalyayana.

13. A blue colour unidentified deity; holds digung (Knife) with vajra in his right hand and skull in left hand near right side of the chest; seated in wrathful form.

14. Amitayus in meditation mudra.

15. Guru Padmasambhava; seated.

16. Buddha in Dharmachara mudra.

17. Birupa : seated with brown body.

18. Buddha in meditation mudra.

19. Saskya Pandita; height-3' 6" width 2'11"

20. Buddha Sakyamuni; Bhumisparsha mudra; new painting.

21. Namtosras : Besides, this temple has two following thankas:

(i) Kongma Nangnga; at the surrounding.
Birupa, Dorje, Chang, Hevajra, Gonpo Dandi, Norchen Kunga Zangpo and Tser Chen Choskyi Lodos.

(ii) Medicine Buddha; pasted on the wall.

(iii) Gonpo Dandi, surrounded by Sakya lamas, Dharma protectors and Bodhisattvas.

(iv) Gonpo Dandi; pasted on the wall.

(v) Namtosras.

(vi) Paldan Lhamo; in the mandala five wrathful deities viz. Turdak, Damzug etc.

(vii) Manjusri; without cotton frame.
Height- 2' 7"
Width –2' 3"

In this temple we can see Buddhist statues as cited below.

1. Buddha.
2. Two lamas.
3. Avalokitesvara.
4. Paldan Lhamo?
5. A lama; probably Sakya order. The Sl.No. 1 to 5 are small statues.
6. Stone carving: Avalokitesvara-four hands, seated.
7. Vajrapani:

   This temple is in a very bad condition and need to preserved immediately without disturbing the wall paintings etc.

8. At last the information about Buddhist statues, paintings, chortens and texts in the Matho monastery as described above though incomple but important source for further research in the monastery.

8

Status and Wall Paintings in Hemis Monastery

Hemis monastery is 45 km. from Leh on the left side of Indus, the most famous institution of Drugpa order in Ladakh. Here follows the details.

Stag stang raspa visited Ladakh during king Singge Namgyal (i.e. in 17th century). Later on the request of king he built this temple at first. It has two precious Buddhist statues as stated below :

1. White Tara :
   Height : 5' 7"
   Called – Dolma Sungjon or a statue which can speak.

2. Stag Stang Ras pa :
   Height – 6'
   Called –Stag Stang Nawang Gyatso.

Wall Paintings on the walls of the Dukhang.

Above the door.

1. Paldan Lhamo : Left side of the door
2. Spalkyi Dorje : Right side of the door

On the left side of the door

3. Carok Dongchan : Face and head Vulture.
4. Gonpo Chagzee : Four hands.

Below the above paintings

5. Gonpo ferocious form.
6. Singge Dongcan : Head lion

7. Chedak : (Tib. Jampal tsedag)
   Heads – Three
   Hands – Six
   Form - Yabyum

Below Chedak

8. Jamyang Karpo : Called white Manjusri.

9. Namgyalma : Left to Chedak.

10. Red Jamyang : Called Red Manjusri.
    At the Centre.

11. Tuskyi Khorlo : Called wheel of life.

On the Wall at the north

12. Stag-stang Nawang gyatso

13. Chepakmet : On the left of Sl.No.12

14. Tilopa : A great Siddha.

15. Naropa : Pupil of Tilopa.

16. Marpa : Pupil of Naropa.

17. Milarepa : Pupil of Marpa.

18. Gyalpo Singge Namgyal.

19. Gyalmo Skalzang Dolma.

20. Namtosras : Deity of Wealth.

21. Luipa : A Siddha.

22. Thirteen ka 'gyad pa lamas.

23. Vajra Dhara : Dorje Chang, the maniestation of Tantric Sakyamuni Buddha.

Central wall facing door

24. Buddha Sakyamuni with his disciples Sariputra and Maudgayana : Centre paintings

25. 12 major events of Buddha surrounded the center painting. Inside the small wall we can see a small White Tara statue in golden colour. On the wall the following Buddhist paintings are depicted.

26. Milarepa

27. Raschungpa

28. Dagpo Lharje : There is no painting on the rest of the wall and being damaged by rain water.

On the right side of the door

29. Guhyasamaj

30. Hevajra

31. Paldan Lhamo

Balkhang

It was built by stag stang Nawang Gyatso when he brought 15 Balti Children who stayed here as lamas. Once on an auspicious ceremony when all these children came out to take *prasad* in a overcrowded mob one Balti child was crashed down. As a result he died on spot. Then stag stang Nawang Gyatso forcasted :

"Though it is a very sad occasion for all of us, it is on the other way good sign for the monastery. In future this establishment will have good strength of lamas and Drugpa tradition flourish throughout in Ladakh."

Thereafter the said child was ceremated and on his name this place named Balti ling.

Dukhang Barma

It is situated in the middle of the monastery and was built by the second incarnation of stag stang Respa named Choskyi Dorje. It has many precious things viz. stupas, statues and paintings. Like other temples it does not have many statues. Here follows the details.

Thrones in this Dukhang

1. Stag Stang raspa.

2. His Holiness Dukchen Rinpoche.

Statues

1. Buddha Sakyamuni : Height- 13': Made of Gold and Copper

2. White Tara : Made of clay; one crown damaged.

3. Dagpo Rinpoche : Made of clay.
   : Called Dagpo Lharje.

4. Choskyi Dorje : Made of copper and silver metals.

5. Chepakmet : Made of herbs and medicinal plants.

6. Dukchen : The sixth incarnation of Dukchen Rinpoche.

7. Padmasambhava with Mandarva and Khanda Ishey Chorgyal : Called Guru cokar made of sandlewood

8. Avalokitesvara : Called Chintamani
   : Infront of Buddha Sakyamuni Statue
   : Made of silver.

9. Avalokitesvara : Made of sandalwood mounted on a pillar.

Scripts

1. Complete Kangyur pothis.

2. Hand written 12 volumes Bum pothis.

3. Printed 12 volumes Bum pothis.

Beams

This Dukhang has 36 wooden beams or pillars each painted with various forms of Buddhas and has Gyamthang.

Wall paintings

Paintings on the varanda wall

1. Yul khor sung : Called Gyaltsen zee named : Dhritarashtra, Zambala, Virudhaka and Virupaksha.

2. Sidpe Khorlo : Called wheel of life.

Above the door

1. Manjusri (Centre)

Right to the Centre painting

2. Avalokitesvara.

3. Singge da

4. Garuda

Left of the Centre painting

5. Vajrapani

6. Green Tara

7. Jamyang Singzon : Manjusri riding on lion.

Left side of the door in the Dukhang

9. Four hands Gonpo

10. Manjusri : Called Chedak

11. Kalcakra : Called Duskhor

Above the Gonpo

12. Janyang Serzang : Right side.

13. Unidentified painting : Left side.

Right side of the door

14. Cakrasamvara

15. Hevajra.

16. Hyegriva : Tib. Tamdin.

17. Vajradhara

Above to These

18. Sarasvati

19. White Jamyang

20. Dharmpala : Faces –Three
    : Arms- Six

Behind the stupas

21. Sixteen Arhats

Dukhang Chenmo

It was built by stang-stang raspas third incarnation during 18th century A.D. His name was Miphan Tsewang Thinles Stangin Migyur. The original wall paintings of this Dukhang damaged. Thereafter paintings on cloth first made later pasted on the walls. During Hemis festival lamas of the monastery perform all concerned rituals here.

Thrones

1. His Holines stag stang Raspa.

2. His Holiness Dukchen Rinpoche.

Mask

1. Pehar gyalpo : He is lha, which captured by Gyaltsras Rinpoche, put in the mask and hanged through the beam. On the 11th day of the 5th month according to Tibetan Calendar lamas of the monastery gather here and offer ritual in the hunour of Pehar gyalpo.

Statues

1. Dugpa Thinles : Riding on wooden horse.
2. stag stang ras pa
3. Kunzing choszang
4. Pagsam Wangbo
5. Thinlas shingta
6. Lingraspa Padma Dorje

Wall Paintings

Right side of the door

1. Standin : Tib.tandin.
2. Khorlodomba

Left side of the door

3. Chepakmet
4. Mazurma Gyalmo (may be Paldan Lhamo)
5. Gonpo Hungzat
6. Rahula.

Right side wall

7. Eight medicine Buddhas
8. Thirty five Buddha
9. Dragpo Lharje
10. Kunkhen Padma Karpo
11. Phagmo Dupa
12. Stag stang ras pa.

13. Mithukpa ; Blue colour holds dorje.

North side wall

14. Sixteen Arhats : In this Dukhang many wall paintings are damaged by rain water.

Chams Lhakhang (Camskhang)

This temple has no wall painting. It was built by stag stang dodul ling in the early 19th century.

Statues of this temple

1. stag stang dodul ling.

2. Buddha : Made of brass
 : Height –8'

3. Avalokitesvara : Made of Marble
 : Height – one foot.

4. Standin : Tandin.

5. Gyalsras Rinpoche.

6. Guru Singge dadol.

7. Stag stang nawang gyatso.

7. Dukchen Rinpoche.

Stupas

One Silver stupa : Height –8'

Lhakhang Cupa

It has ten pillars and named after as cupa Lhakhang. Today it doesn't have any pillar and has eleven-headed Avalokitesvara, the main statue. There are many clay and sandalwood statues as shown below.

1. Buddha : Infront of the main statue; made of sandalwood.

2. Lopon Cokhor sum : Made of Sandalwood.

3. Four handed Avalokitesvara : Made of Sandalwood.

4. Rigsumgonpo : Made of clay

5. Four handed Avalokitesvara : Made of silver.

6. Thang Thong Gyalpo.

7. Co lokesvara

8. Yuthog yontan gonpo.

9. Dorje Chang ; Made of Clay

10. Avalokitesvara : Named tonyot zagspa

11. Dorje Sempa : Height –6'

12. stag stang raspa

Zimsung Padma Odling

It was built according to the advise of stag stang Padma odling and has following statues.

1. Eleven-headed Avalokitesvara : Main Statues.

2. Chagdor (or Vajrapani)

3. Manjusri

4. Small Statues of Avalokitesvara on the above.

5. Unidentified lama

6. Buddha.

In the almirah

7. Opakmet

8. Karmapa Zanak

Left to right

9. Dolma : Made of gold

10. A lama : Made of clay

11. Co-Buddha: Made of Sandalwood

12. Dolma : Made of clay (below above)

12. A Lama : Unidentified.

13. A Lama : Unidentified.

14. A Lama : Unidentified

Zimsung Phunchok Spalkhang Statues

1. Neve Srachen gyat : Made of sandalwood. They are-

(1) Jamyang

(2) Chagna Dorje

(3) Avalokitesvara

(4) Sai Ningbo

(5) Timpar Nampar sel

(6) Namkhe Ningpo

(7) Chamba

(8) Kunduzang

Lhamo Khang statues

1. kunkhen Padma Karpo : Made of gold & silver

2. Dolma : Made of clay Beside it has various precious thankas popular among them paldan Lhamo Thanka.

Zimsung Some Status

1. Lopon Padma : Made of silver
2. Buddha
3. Dordan ma
4. Ka 'gyad Lamas : 6" in height
   : All made of clay

   There is one throne of stag stang ras pa

Guru Lhakhang Statue

It has Lopon Padma Zunas main statue, popularly called Padma-Sambhava Khan sum zil non. It was built by Nawang Tsering, Tiapa during 1983-84. It is about 31' in height.

Gunkhang statues

In this temple main statues are Gonpokagyat

(i) Four hands Gonpo

(ii) Two hands Gonpo

(iii) Six hands Gonpo

(iv) Gonpo Carok Dongcan

(v) Gonpo Pen

(vi) Gonpo Zal Zeepa

(vii) Gonkar

(viii) Gonpokhetapa

Besides it has Gonpokagyat thankas.

In conclusion, Hemis monastery has very precious statues and wall paintings, unfortunately many wall paintings being damaged by rain water. Therefore, rest of them needed to be preserved carefully.

References

1. Janyang Gyaltsen (ed.) : *The History of Ladakh Monasteries*. All Ladakh Gonpa Society publication, 1995:149-160.

2. Nawang Tsering : 'The Monasteries of Hemis, Chemde and Dagthang' without date : 12-38.

9

Sachi Chosling Gon (Tib. Sa-spyi-chos-gling-dgon) : A Geluk-pa Monastery

Name : Sachi Chosling gon is popularly known Sap gonpa.[1]

Approach : The monastery is about 190 km from Leh in Kargil district.[2] By taxi we can go upto the gonpa. It was built in 19th century.

Administration : It is under the administrative control of Likir monastery [3]. According to the Geluk-pa tradition[4], the Likir gonpa welfare society sends one or two lamas to look after the monastery and religious activities in Sapi[5] and its adjoining areas.[6]

Statues : It has the following Buddhist statues.

1. Avalokitesvara[7] :
   Eyes – 1000
   Hands – 1000
   Heads – Eleven

2. Gyalva Tsong-Khapa (Tib. rgyal ba tsong-ka pa)[8]

3. Avalokitesvara (Tib.byan ras gzit phyag-drug)[9]
   Hands – Six
   Colour – white

Thanka : It is called scroll painting and usually painted on the piece of canvas. It is put in Lukewarm water with glue and lime to wet. In order to dry it, stretched on the thin wooden square frame. Its surface is rubbed with smooth object until it becomes ready for painting. The main guidelines are drawn first just as the border lines, a central perpendicular and two diagonals and so according to the figures to be sketched. In this monastery such following paintings are available:

1. Avalokitesvara.
2. Amitabha[10]

Pothis : Each monastery in Ladakh represents kaya, vaka and citta. Pothis are the symbol of vaka. Here we find the following Buddhist texts.

1. Kangyur[11]
2. Dode-skalzang
3. Zong-dus
4. Padma-Thangyik

Chorten : It is the symbol of citta. In this gonpa I saw only one Namgyal Chorten[12] made of wood.

Rituals items :

1. Dorje
2. Tilu (Bell)
3. Bowls (water offering bowls)
4. Lamps (Oil lamps)

Notes and References

1. Sapi gonpa : Tib. sa-pi gon-pa.

2. Kargil
   Lat. 34° 34'
   Long. 76° 11'
   Elev. 8,787 feet.

   It is the district headquarters of Kargil district. This district has Suru, Dras, Zangskar and Purig Valleys.

3. Likir monastery: It is across the Indus River from Alchi and about 10 km north of Saspol or 52 km west of Leh. It was built in the time of Lhachen Gyalpo during 11th century. Later during 15 Century refounder under the Geluk-pa tradition. Cf. Finegan, Jack: 'Tibet-A Dreamt of Image', Tibet House, 1986:192.

4. Geluk-pa tradition : This tradition was founded by Tsong-Khapa.

   During Dragpa Bunde regime two ascetics arrived in Ladakh, who had been sent by Tsong-Khapa and were carrying a copy made personally by Tsong-khapa of the Amitayurdhyana Sutra, a work of meditation on the Tathagata Amitayus. Tsong-Khapa had told his emissaries to give the book to either of two persons, either to the one called Drogpa Bumde or Dragpa Bum. Drapa Bum was at that time in Nubra. The two ascetics came there first but, when they entered the presence of the king, he paid no attention to them. Accordingly they went on to Leh, and there on the morrow Dragpa Bumde admitted his *darbar* any who wished to come. When the two ascetics came into his presence the king rose and went to meet them, they made over the present of the book from Tsong-Khapa. But in my opinion they offered Amitayus statue to the king. However, king was delighted with it. Later he built Spituk monastery and the gift which he received from Tsong-Kapa emissiaries in the monastery. Cf.Finegan, Jack; *Op.cit*:170 and Jina, Prem Singh: '*Thiksey monastery in Ladakh Himalaya*; Satguru Pub, New Delhi, 2006.

5. Sa-pi. It is a village in Kargil district.

6. Jina, Prem Singh : Ladakh: The Land and People; Indus Pub.Co.

7. Avalokitesvara : (Tib. spyan ras gzigs).

He is a manifestation of Amitabha, is shown in white colour, has Om Mani Padme Hum as his mantra, is the special protector of Tibet, and is incarnate in king Songtsan Gonpa. He has many forms. The form with eleven heads is explained by the story that when Avalokitesvara looked down upon the many beings in need of deliverance in the hell of Yama, the god of death, his head broke into ten pieces out of his great compassion; these were put together by his spiritual father Amitabha; thus in the figure there are nine gentle faces arranged in three tiers of three each, above that one wrathful face and 'at the top' the head of Amitabh, thus making eleven heads in all. With his thousand arms. Cf.Finegan, Jack, *op.cit.*:130-31.

8. Gyalva Tsong-Khapa (Tib.rgyal ba tsong-ka-pa): He was born in 1357 in the district of Tsong-kha in the vicinity of Kokonor lake in Amdo, where in 1578 Kumbum monastery was founded. In 1409, he founded his own monastery called Ganden, and he became the head of his own order. From the name of the monastery the order was first known as the Ribo Ganden-pa, later popular by Geluk-pa. Cf. Finegan, Jack; 'Tibet : A Dreamt of Image, *op.cit.*:100-101.

9. Avalokitesvara (Tib.byan ras gzit phyag-drug): The six arms Avalokitesvara is known as Padmapani. He holds the lotus as Amoghapasha. Cf.Finegan, Jack; *op.cit*:130.

10 Amitabah : He is the Buddha of infinite light and is one of the Dhayani Buddha, embodiment of compassion. Cf. 'Tara; 'An exhibition of Rare Buddhsit Thanks'; CIBS, Leh; 2003:20.

11. Kangyur : Tib. bke'gyur Pron. Kanjur. It means 'translations of the word bka' or Buddha speech', and contains the whole Teravada and Mahayana literature, as well as the Tantras which are the foundation of the Vajrayana. Cf. Finegan, Jack; *op. cit.*:14-15.

12. Namgyal Chorten : When Buddha expressed his desire to take parinirvana, his pupils felts sorry. They requested him not to take nirvana. Buddha then agreed with them, and stayed some days. Bhikshus later' under the leadership of 'go-mi-cum-da' constructed a chorten which later known as Namgyal chorten.

10

Two Small Buddhist Temples in Kharbu

In Kharbu two small gonpas were built in co-operation with villagers, here follows the details.

Kharbu Ringchen ling gonpa

This gonpa was built by Lama Konchok Tondup in 1864. In Tibetan language pronounce as mkhar bu dgon rin chen ling. Kharbu villagers didn't collect sufficient money till 1964, hence no major renovation was undertaken. In 1965 they again went to collect donation. This time good amount was collected. In the same year after meeting, villagers decided to build a new gonpa infront of the old building. In the completion of the gonpa, lamas offered prayer for seven days, at the end threw storma. New gonpa was purified by rituals and all the statues from the old monastery was transferred to this shrine. The Buddhist images of this gonpa is cited below[1].

1.	Avalokitesvara[2]	: Centre statue
		: Hands – one thousand
		: Eyes – one thousand
2.	Skyoba[3]	: Right side of the center statue
3.	Padmasambhava[4]	
4.	Buddha[5]	

5. Namgyal Chorten[6]

In 1971 Kharbur Namgyal Society collected donation and constructed Namgyal chorten. It is decorated by precious metals and stones. Thereafter stong chot[7] rituals performed by the lamas for the welfare of human beings. In 1980, Kangyur[8] and stangyur pothis were purchased for the gonpa.

Kharbu Lhakhang

Buddhist temple at Kharbu village is known as 'mkhar bu lha khang gsang sdays chos gling'. In 1871 village Lha Lhasar gyalpo[9] forcasted, "for the welfare of this village Tashi Tanphel[10] will build a temple". Accordingly, with the help of Tashi Wangdan,[11] Tashi, Tanphel built the Kharbu Buddhist temple.[12]

The temple was constructed. later without water and other basic amenities, it was not properly look after by the concerned authority. One day one vulture all of a sudden flew to Kharbu valley from north side and Lhasar gyalpo appeared from the east. After some time Lha Lhasar forecasted, "If you need water and stones for the monastery you have to pray your village deity".[13]

Villagers did the same and offered prayers for the welfare of their community and for the temple. Lha listened their prayer and by his spiritual power the land was irrigated by water and stones. Consequently the temple was rebuilt. It took complete five years.

The following statues are installed in the monastery

1. Maitreya[14] : Height – one Storey i.e. about 12'
2. Amitayaus[15] : Height –12'
3. Avalokitesvara : Hands – one thousand
Eyes – one thousand
4. Skyoba Jigten Gonpo: Founder of Drigung order

5. Rigsum gonpo[16].

6. Chepagmet (or Chepakmet)[17]

7. Six kinds of Padmasambhava[18]

8. Gelong ma Palmo[19]

9. Sera gyal po[20]

10. Vajrapani[21]

11. Zangpo dul zot[22]

Wall Paintings

The shrine has the following wall paintings :

1. Paintings of traditional lamas of Drugpa K'agyud[23]

2. Sixteen Arhats[24]

3. Thirty five Buddhas[25]

Wall paintings on the walls of Dukhang

Here follows the beautiful paintings on the wall of the prayer hall.

1. Eight kinds Indian Acharyas[26]

2. Twelve kinds Buddhas[27]

3. Paintings based on Gelam Kesar[28]

4. One hundred various forms of Buddha and Bodhisattvas

5. Eight kinds of chortens[29]

6. Zangdo palri[30]

7. Milarepa[31]

8. Carung Khasor[32]

9. Eight Medicine Buddhas[33]

10. Five Dhyani Buddhas[34]

11. Phagmo lha nga[35]

12. Twenty one Dolmas[36]

13. Canrazik Dova tukdol[37]

14. Mithukpa.[38]

Gonkhang

In the Gonkhang temple of this monastery has the following Buddhist statues.

1. Dorjechang Tib.rdo rje'achang.

2. Gonpo-Hands : Four Tib.mgon po phyag bzhi pa

3. Apchi (Tib. aphyi)

4. Dechok (Tib.bde mchog drill bu)

Paintings of this temple

In this temple we can see various Buddhist deities depicted on the walls as cited below.

1. Man nag gyud pe lo gyus: Tib. man ngay brgyud p'ai lo rgyus. Depicted on the wall at the north.

2. Padmasambhava. Tib. guru drag po with mandala. Shown on the wall at the east.

3. Dugpa K'agyud's various deities are painted on the west side wall.

Religious texts

The monastery has good collection of Kangyur pothis, brought here from Tibet.

Zimsung (Tib.gzims chang)

Initially Zimsung was built for the head lama of the monastery during 1952. Thereafter Tondup and Khanpo of the monastery re-built this in 1984.

In conclusion, Kharbu has two small Buddhist temples which are very well preserved by a small group of Buddhist population. Earlier Kharbu to Kargil Buddhist had many temples, but due to the Islamic influence in this region during 15th century and onwards maximum Buddhist families were converted into Islam as a result Muslim population increased very fast and within three centuries all villages between Kharbu to Kargil dominated by Muslims and Buddhist temples were either destroyed or may be converted into mosques.

During 18th century Drigung pa lamas endeavoured to propagate Buddhism in Purig side, but only a few visited there and could not convence the villagers very well. However, those who visited Aryan region viz., Da, Bema, Hanu, Garkon, etc. were got success in this stream.

Notes and References

1. Jamyang Gyaltsan (ed.) 'The History of Ladakh Monasteries', All Ladakh Gonpa Society, Leh, 1995:674.

2. Avalokitesvara : Tib. spyan ras gzigs phyag stong spyan stong.

   He is the Buddha of compassion and the chief Budhisttva of Mahayana Buddhism. The eleven heads and one thousand arms consists eye on each palm. Budhisattva in fact years ago promised to attain enlighenment until all sentient beings attain enlightenment. It is said when Avalokitesvara looked down upon the many beings in need of deliverance in the hell of Yama, the god of death, his head broke into ten pieces out of his great compassion. Finegan, jack: 'Tibet:A Dreamt of Image', Tibet House, New Delhi;1986:130.

3. Skyopa : Tib. skyob pa pron Jigten Gonpo. He was the student of Phakmotru-pa and was the founder of Drigung- pa a sub-order of Kagyud pa. This order was named after Drigung monastery, which was established by Jigten Gonpo in 1179 about 128 km northeast of Lhasa. Cf. Finegan,Jact; *Op.cit.*: 96.

4. Padmasambhava : Tib. guru rin po che. He was the great mystic saint from India who had tremendous miraculous powers. He brought Buddhist Tantra in Tibet in the 8th century. Later he subdued the local deities and demons who were obstructing the construction Samyas monastery: Lobzang Tsewang: ' Sakyamuni', CIBS, 2001 : 26.

5. Buddha: Tib. thub dba or Sakyamuni Buddha. In 6th century B.C., he descended to the world to show the right path to the fortunate beings, so that they may attain freedom from the cycle of existence. After attaining enlightenment he delivered religious sermons for the benefit of all sentient beings. Cf. Lobzang Tsewang; *op. cit:* 20.

6. Namgyal chorten : Tib. rnam rgyal mchot rten. This chorten was built after the Parinirvana of Tathagata under the leadership of 'Go-mi-cum-do'.

7. Stong chot: Tib. stong mchod.

8. Kangyru : Tib. bk'a 'agyur rin po che. The Kangyur means translations of the word bka' word or speech i.e. of the Buddha. It contains the whole Theravada and Mahayana literature, as well as the Tantras which are the foundation of the Vajrayana. Finegan, Jack; *op.cit.* : 14-15.

9. Lhaser gyalpo : Tib. lha bse ral rgyal po.

10. Tashi Tanphel: Tib. bkris bstan 'aphel.

11. Tashi Wangdan ; Tib. bris dbang ltan.

12. Jamyang Gyaltsan (ed); *op.cit*: 675.

13. *Ibid.*

14. Maitreya : Among Ladakhi Buddhists he is popularly known as Future Buddha or chamba. It is said that a time will come in future when Buddha teaching will be disappeared from the world. He will then come down in the earth and will establish Buddhism on the line Buddha teachings.

15. Amitayus: Long life Buddha, both hands in meditation mudra and an urn resting on his palms, contains pills of longevity. He is in golden colour possessing on face, two hands and two legs. In Ladakh Amitayus figure erects in red colour.

16. Rigsum gonpo : The three following images all together called Rigsum gonpo:
    (i) Avalokitesvara (White colour)
    (ii) Vajrapani (Blue colour)
    (iii) Manjusri (Red colour).

17. Chepakmet : In Sanskrit called Amitayus, Please see Ref. No.15.

18. Six kinds of Padmasambhava: Tib. 'agro ba drug gi gu ru drug. Generally Padmasambhava manifested in eight forms viz. (1) Guru Sakya Senge (2) Guru Padmasambhava (3) Guru Nyima Ozer (4) Guru Senge Dradok (5) Guru Dorje Doloe (6) Guru Tsekye Dorje (7) Guru Padma Gyalpo (8) Guru Loden Chokse.

19. Gelong ma Palmo : Tib. dge slong ma dpal mo.

20. Sera gyal po : Tib. se ra rgyal po.

21. Vajrapani : Tib. phyag rdor or phyag ma rdo rje, holder of the thunderbolt is a manifestation of Akshobya, and is usually shown as dark blue in colour with a crown of skulls and holding dorje.

22. Zango dul zot : 'abyung po' adul byed.

23. Traditional lamas of Drugpa K'agyud : Tib.byang dos su 'abri gung bk'a brgyud kyi gdan rabs bla brgyud.

24. Sixteen Arhats: Tib. shar dos su gnas brtan bcu drug. The group of these sixteen Arhats is believed to have been entrusted by Sakyamuni Buddha with the continuing task of protecting the doctrine of Buddha.

25. Thirty five Buddhas : Tib. nub dos su ltung bshags kyi sangs rgyas so lnga.

26. Eight kinds Indian Acharyas: Tib. rbyan drug mchog gnyis; on the north side wall they are depicted. They are:
    (1) Kru sgsub.
    (2) Thog med
    (3) 'aphags pa lha
    (4) dbyig gnyen
    (5) phyogs glang
    (6) chos grags
    (7) yon tan 'od
    (8) Sh'akya 'od

27. Twelve kinds Buddhas : Tib. mdzad pa bchus gnyis ; on the left wall they are depicted in various forms.

28. Gelam kesar. Tib. bling ge sar. In Ladakh folk songs and folk stories Gelan Kesar acted as a hero and great warrior.

29. Eight kinds chortens : Tib bde gshegs mchod rten brgyad. They are painted below the Buddhas and Bodhisattvas. The chortens are chang chup' Lhababs' sgo-mang, chos-thrul pad-spung, Fn-dum, Namgyal and Nyang Das.

30. Zongdo palri: Tib. zangs mdog dpal ri 'ai. On the wall east-west it is painted.

31. Milarepa : Tib. Mila ripa. He is shown at the south of the door. Marpa was a good mahasidddha of tantra. Later he transmitted this tradition to his disciple Milarepa, who later became most famous yogi and poet in Tibet.

32. Carung Khasor : Tib. bya rung khas shor; shown above the door.

33. Eight Medicine Buddhas : Tib. sman lha bde gshegs brgyad. On the right side of the door they are depicted (1) sh'akya thub pa (2) sman gyi bla (3) mngon mkhyen rgya po (4) shos sgrags rgya mtsho (5) mya ngan med mchog dped (6) gser bzang dri med (7) sgra dbyangs rgyal po (8) mtshan legs yongs bsgrags depal.

34. Five Dhyani Buddhas : Tib. rgyal ba rig slnga; on the right side wall of the door they are depicted viz. (1) rnam par snag mdzad (2) mi skyod pa (3) rin chen 'abyung ldan (4) snang ba mth'a yas (5) don yod grub pa.

35. Phagmo lha nga : Tib. phag mo lha nga; on the right side wall of the door they are depicted.

36. Twenty one Dolmas : Tib. sgrol ma nyer gcig. On the north west of the door. Dolma is shown in twenty one forms.

37. Canrazik Dova tukdol : Tib. spyam ras gzigs 'agro ba drug sgrol. On the north of the door he is shown. The Buddha of compassion is called canrazik or Avalokitesvara. He is the chief Buddhisattva of Mahayana Buddhism.

38. Mithukpa : Tib . mi'a grugs pa. On the north of the door he is shown. He is a form of Buddha , blue colour holds dorje.

11

Phugtal Gonpa

This gonpa is an old one was founded by Phagspa Sesrab[1] in 1070 A.D. In those days Lotsava Rinchen Zangpa who was in his tour for propagating Buddhism throughout in Western Tibet. Phagspa Sesrab was also influenced by him and accordingly put Phugtal gonpa under Kadampa order.

In 15th Century Cang Sems Sherab Zangpo[2] visited Ladakh. He established Thiksey monastery[3] in Central Ladakh. Thereafter with the kind support of villagers, Lama population gradually increased in this monastery. He, then started to teach them Buddhist philosophy and logic. He implemented strict Vinayic rules and regulations in the monastery. As he got full confidence in his disciples and about the smoth functioning of monastic decipline, he decided to visit Zanskar to propagate Geluk pa order. In 1457 he arrived Phugtal monastery. Thereafter, re-established the same under the Gelukpa order.[4] Today it is functioning under Gelukpa tradition and has about 120 lamas. The monastery has Gonkhang, Dukhang, stonba Lhakhang and many rooms for lamas, Fig.11.1.

Gonkhang : This is the oldest temple of the monastery. It is decorated by Buddhist statues and thankas given as below.

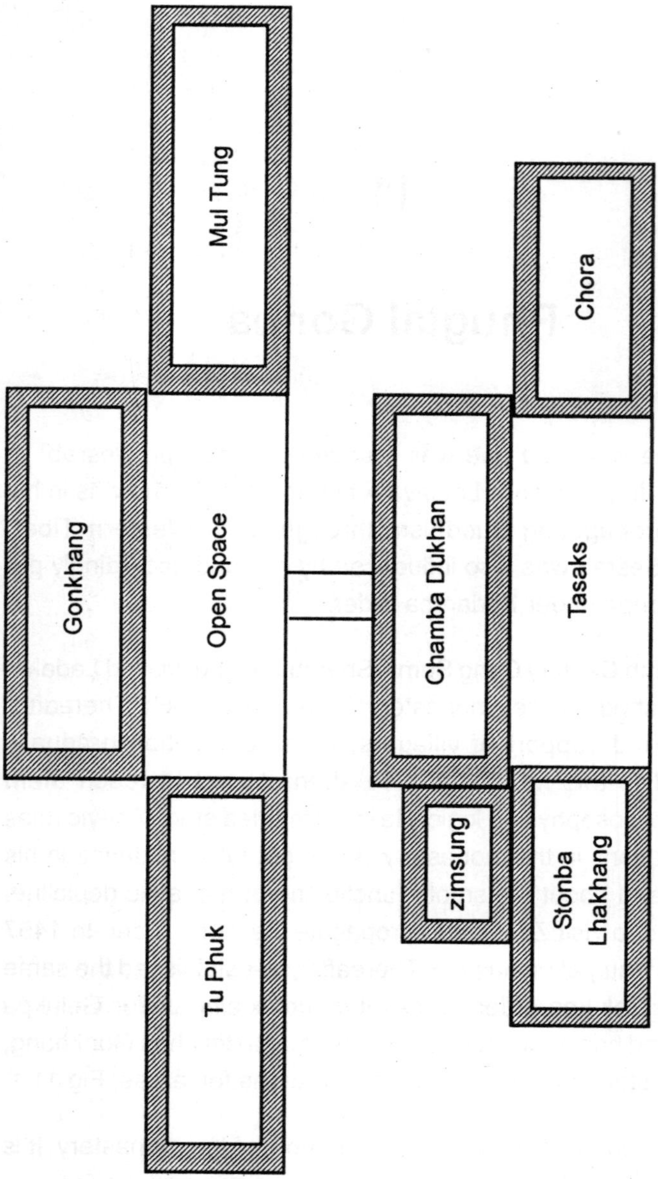

Fig. 11.1. Temples in Phugtal Gonpa (Zanskar) Not to scale.

1. Gonpo: Statue Height-6'

2. Lha cuksum : Thankas
: Thirteen in number.

3. Lhamo[5] : Thanka:
: Height –5'

4. Lama Chotpe Chokzing : Thanka
: Height – 6'

5. Sangdu Kinggor : Thanka height-5'

Chamba lhakahang has Chamba statue[6] made of clay. It is about 11 feet in height. Similarly in Stonba Lhakhang has about 7' Buddha statue.

Sokpo Galdan Tsewang

It is said while entering in upper Ladakh Sokpo Galdan Tsewang passed through Zankar. He saw Phughal gonpa on his way and decided to capture monastery property. To see his bad intention the main doors of the monastery were closed down by the lamas. Some soldiers of the Galdan Tsewang[7] army opened fire, three bullets strucked the doors but didn't harm. In the mean while one Sokpo soldier threw rope and tried to climb to gonpa from back side, Lamas were not aware of this. Paldan Lhamo appeared before lamas and said:

"Your enemy is entering in the gonpa from backside by rope. Cut the rope and kill him, otherwise he may harm the gonpa".

All lamas then went to backside of the gonpa and killed him by stones, and saved the gonpa.

Administration

This monastery is under Likir. Nari Rinpoche is the head of the monastery and functioning according to the Gelukpa tradition. To look after the monastery, lamas of the monastery occupy different posts according to seniority in the following way

Nari Rinpoche
|
Lhopon
|
Umzat
|
Uchung
|
Gyeskyos
|
Nirpa (Senior)
|
Nirpa (Junior)

Cunzung (Young lama)	Cunzung (young lama)	Cunzung (young lama)

Ritual Ceremony

In the monastery lamas do not sit ideal. They are engaged in various rituals prayers thoughout the year according to the following calendar (Table : 11.1).

Table 11.1: Ritual Calendar in Phugtal Gonpa

Sl.No.	*Name of the ritual*	*Calendar*	*Day*
1.	Tsechu	During Feb.	2
2.	Smonllam[8]	-Feb-	2
3.	Rinpoche Zabdan	-Feb-	2
4.	Chiksum Chotpa	-Feb-	2
5.	Gustor[9]	-Feb-	2
6.	Zeve Wanchok	-May-	5

(Contd.)

(Contd.Table 11.1)

Sl.No.	*Name of the ritual*	*Calender*	*Day*
7.	Sangdus	-May-	3
8.	Yarnes[11]	-Oct-	15
9.	Nungnas[10]	-Oct-	15
10.	Zigjed prayer	-	7
11.	Golden Nanchot[12]	-	15

The above rituals are performed by lamas in Chamba Dukhang. On the occasion of the concerned ritual, lamas gathered in the above Dukhang early morning. According to the direction of the Khanpo, Umzet starts prayer with ritual musical instruments. During the prayer salty Ladakhi tea is served four times in a day and two times food (i.e. in the morning and noon) is given to lamas.

In Gustor lamas of the monastery with the direction of Champspon perform cham. During Nungnas villagers take fast, come to gonpa and offer prayer. This time gonpa authority serve them tea and perform ritual prayers for their welfare. Sometime for the intertainment some groups arrange dance and drama.

This gonpa has good collection of Buddhist texts and has 108 volumes of Kangyur and Stangyur pothis. During 15th Century after the establishment of Tagmo and Thiksey monasteries in central Ladakh. Diskyit and Incha monasteries in Nubra valley, Cang sems sherab zangpo came down to Zanskar for the propagation of Geluk pa order. In his last days he stayed in Phugtaal monastery. His body is preserved in a chorten in this temple.

Notes and References

1. Phagspa sesrab : He was a lama probably influence by Kadampa order founded by Atisa.

2. Cang sems shesrab zangpo. He was a disciple of Tsong Khapa a founder of Geluk pa order came Ladakh during 15th century along with his assistant. First time when he met Dragpa Bumde, the king of Ladakh, he was not given good response by the king. In the second time king gave full respect and requested him to establish his monastery in Ladakh.

3. Thiksey monastery : Tib. Tikse and is situated at a distance of 5 km from Shey on a prominent hill on the right bank of the Indus with a sweeping view from Spituk in the northwest to the ravine that leads to Hemis in the southeast. Cf. Finegan Jack: 'Tibet-A dreamt of Image', Tibet House, New Delhi, 1986:201.

4. Gelukpa order: In 1409 Tsong Khapa founded Ganden monastery in Tibet. From the name of the monastery it was first known as Ribo Ganden pa, from its derivation from the tradition of Atisa and Drom it was called the New Kamplampa, and then Geluk-pa. Cf.Finegan jack; *op.cit.*101.

5. Lhamo (Tib. Paldan Lhamo) : The Glorious Goddess, is one of the most important protectors of the Geluk pa order of Buddhism and the guardian of Lhasa. History tells us that she was the jewel protector, extremely aggressive and was the custodian of religious properties and was initiated by Chagna Dorje and was given the name Dorje Naljorma.

6. Chamba statue : Maitreya. The king one. A Mahabodhisattva and the Buddhisattva who will be the Manushi Buddha of future age. The Buddha to be who will show the way to nirvana. He is a Bodhisattva who is equally respected by the Theravadists and Mahayanists.

7. Galdan Tsewang. He was a Mongol Lama Calleg Tsang and was resided at Galden, therefore popularly known Galdan Tsang. Later he turned layman and soon became the head of Mongol tribe as well as Tibetan army, thereafter entered into Ladakh and defected Ladakh army near Pang-gong lake then arrived Basgo. Cf. Francke, A.H.: 'A History of Western Tibet' 1995:106.

8. Smonllam: According to Tibetan calendar it is on 1st month at 14-15.

9. Gustor (or Phugtal Gustor) : It is on 28-29 on the 12th month of the Tibtan calendar.

10. Nungnas : It falls on 3rd of the 6th month of the Tibetan calendar.

11. Yarnes : From 15-30 of the 6th month according to Tibetan calendar lamas of the monastery go for yarnes.

12. Galdan Namchot :13-27 of the 10th month according to Tibetan calendar.

12

Some Renowned Lamas of Ladakh

Tsulthim Nima :

Tsulthim Nima was born in 1790 at Saspol village, Leh district, Ladakh. His house name was Khache. Since early childhood he belief on the philosophy of nonviolence. It is said once a wounded bird fell infront of him. Tsulthim Nima was then three years old, immediately catched the bird, gave water, then hid in a safe place. After sometimes, when bird was allright, he released it.

Lama Lozang Gelak Ishey Dragpa gave him name 'Stenzin Tsewang' at the age of 5 years. After two years he went to Gyeshes Mila and listened *Skyabdo & Gyadas teachings*. His father Lozang Tashi was educated person, he had a good knowledge of Bodhi, thus leared Bodhi language from him. His mother Jamskyit was a simple lady, he learned simplicity and honesty from her. Subsequently, from these characters he became popular among village community and was known as 'khache pa no no'. In those days *shyammas* used to go to Chang-Thang or even upto Tibet for trade. At the age of 12 years a shyamma trader came to him, he was very much influenced by his honesty, and asked:

"No-No Khacha pa, I need a helper, would you like to do this job."

"What will be my job."

"You have to go with me to Chang-thang and look after my goods and animals only."

"O.K. I'm ready to go with you."

Tsulthim Nima became servant of Shyamma trader, along with him went to Chang-thang. Soonafter with his sharp mind he learned business techniques and started his own business. As a result he often visited upto Rudok for pashmina and exchanged the same with traders at Leh market.

He was a honest businessman. Once in Rudok under agreement he purchased pashmina from 60 Dochet, later found it excess which cost one *Doschet*. On the next day he again met the trader and returned excess pashmina. The trader was very much pleased with him, hence became famous among Tibetan traders.

In those day Pashmina and wool were transported from Chang-Thang and Rudok to Leh by yaks and sheep. These animals then sold into the hands of buchers at Leh. Tsulthim Nima was not happy with this tradition. He established a new system underwhich traders had to hire animals from Chang-thang or area concerned, after unloading they had to return them.

Tsulthim Nima was the only child of his parents, who wanted their son should stay with them. His father decided to marry his son. Tsulthim Nima was only 18 years old. He married him with a girl of his village Yang-zom of a *Tozo-tshe* family. After sometimes his mother died, later his teacher Gyeshes Mila also died. He felt sorry and thought to become lama, but for the sake of his family, he was bound to return to Chang-Thang for business. However, was inclined to follow Buddhist tradition in his life. He started reading *Lam-rim thongme Lozong*, time and again he went to Lama Lozang Stanzin and listened from him *Phakpo chugze chenpo* teachings, later he also endeavoured to practice Bodh-vinaya. At the age of 29 years he got a son. When child was 5 years old, he donated him to Likir monastery as a lama. *Lama Lozang Stanzin* named him Ishey Rabgyas, under his guidance he studied Bodhi language.

Though Tsulthim Nima was born in a poor family, by virtue of his head work and honesty he gathered good property. As came to know, his father died, he realized the truth of suffering. At the age of 30 years, he left his house and family, didn't bother for his property, went towards West Tibet. After twenty days tough and long journey he reached Tholing, later met the abbot of Tashigang monastery, became monk and named 'Tshulthim Nima'.

After sometimes Lama Tshulthim Nima expressed his desire to visit to Mount Kailash and Mansarovar Lake. His teacher and abbot of the Tashigang monastery happily allowed him and said:

"Don't forget Vinaya rules and regulations."

Lama Tshulthim Nima promised to practice Vinaya strictly. Thereafter, went towards the path of Mount Kailash and Manasarovar. At Manasarovar lake he retreat in a nearby *Juthul-Phuk* cave for three months. One day he saw his sister 'Garmo' along with some Ladakhis infront of his cave. Later she requested him to return to Ladakh. Tshulthim Nima didn't agree. She again requested him to accompany her at least upto Tashigang monastery. Tsulthim Nima couldn't deny her this time and went with her party upto the monastery. Here 'Garmo' requested his teacher to persuade her brother to go to Ladakh.

Later on the advice of his teacher Tsulthim Nima joined his party and returned to Ladakh. He met his wife Yang-zom, who later became Bhikshuni.

Tsulthim Nima fully dedicated himself for religious works, staying a few days in Leh, he went to his native place and constructed Zong-lung cave in between Saspol and Likir. He went for meditation for six months. Thereafter, thought to study Buddhist Philosophy texts under the guidance of some learned scholars. He didn't find such scholars in Ladakh. Therefore, once again went to Tashigang monastery, under the guidance of *Khen Rinpoche* studied Buddhist Philosophy. His teacher later advised him to return to Ladakh for the propagation of Buddhism. This time, Lama Tsenzin Nima, Tenzin Gyatso and Tenzin Tsulthim accompanied him and assisted in religious works.

Coming after at Leh, he went to his native land Saspol, then to Rizong. In those days Rizong had only a small Lha-Khang. Therefore, Tsulthim Nima decided to construct a big and disciplined monastery. In this connection he made several visits to the Rizong. Soonafter, he selected Ribo-chen mountain for this purpose. He visited Hemi Shukpacan, Alchi, Saspol and other neighbouring villages for donation, asked villagers to help him for the monastery construction. Villagers happily accepted his request. In the following year villagers as volunteers came forward and worked for the same. Two Dukhangs each of four beams were constructed within a short time. Gradually some rooms for lamas were also being constructed. According to Gelukpa tradition Dukhangs were decorated by Buddhist statues and frescos. Tshulthim Nima re-named the monastery 'Chang-chup-Ling.' Thereafter, he went for meditation along with some monks. During winter he arranged a place for *gso-sbyong* recitations. As a result of his hard work lama population in the monastery had been increased. To maintain discipline in the monastery he constituted the following rules and regulations:[1]

1. No monk is allowed to leave the hermitage except in case of sickness.

2. No monk is allowed to sleep his cell spreading a bedding at night.

3. No monk is allowed to touch any such objects which have been brought by a woman including one's own mother or sister.

4. No monk is allowed to leave his cell except for fetching water either before sunrise or after sunset.

5. No monk is allowed to keep any possession even worth the value of a needle, except for his religious books.

6. No monk is allowed to make fire privately in his cell.

7. Any kin of offering, even a single slice of bread which one has received from as *dana* (donation) must equally be shared by all the inmates of the hermitage.

8. The Boundary of the hermitage is marked by three types of fences and no women is allowed to sleep even at the outermost boundary of the hermitage.

9. In case of slightest suspicion regarding a major offence committed by a monk, the person in question will immediately be shut out from the hermitage.

The monks in the monastery later followed the above cited rules strictly. As a result within a short time Rizong monastery became famous throughout in Ladakh for its disciplined nature, devotees accordingly visited the monastery with offerings. The king of Ladakh also offered handsome money for the development of the same.

In 1834 Wazir Zorawar Singh invaded Ladakh, many monasteries on the way to Leh were being plundered by his army. Rizong remained safe, many villagers took refuge. The young generation of that time preferred this monastery to be ordained. Lama population suddenly increased, Tsulthim Nima didn't bother, instead he made a rule, "no monk in his monastery is allowed to earn money by performing rituals in the villages. As a result total money in cash and kind thus earned will be deposited at the monastery account." By virtue of this tradition monks in the monastery were able to live happily and regularly paid their attention in meditation as well in studies. To increase income source Tshulthim Nima gave monastery land on lease to the villagers and with the hardworking of monks he turned barren land of Yang Thang into cultivated ground.

Tshulthim made a valuable contribution in the renovattion of important Buddhist monuments in Ladakh. He raised funds for this purpose as cited below.[2]

1. Maitreya statue of Red monastery at Leh, built by king Bum-lde.

2. Sakya Buddha statue of Shey palace, three stories in height.

3. Gigantic stupa near Shey palace, erected by king Deldan Namgyal.

After sometimes, Lama Tsulthim Nima decided to visit Nubra valley and propagated the roots of his tradition. He founded Samstanling (Tib. bsam-rtan-gling) monastery at the same discipline of Rizong monastery. Now, his attention was concentrated on the spiritual development of Rizong and Samstanling monasteries. He always insisted his disciples to take care sila and should remain pure like gold, in order to do this they should go for meditation time to time. To give strength to the above mission he used to go for meditation. At the age of 70, he passed away at Rizong monastery. His ashes kept in a sealed urn, later a stupa was made on it and placed in the Dukhang of the same monastery.[3]

In conclusion, Tsulthim Nima was a massenger of peace and harmony. In 1834 when General Zorawar Singh invaded Ladakh he advised Stokpa Kalon Dorje Namgyal and king Tondup Tenzin to settle down war in peaceful manner so that Ladakhi Buddhist art and culture, could be preserved. Thus, he dedicated his whole life for the preservation and promotion of Buddhism in Ladakh.

Tagna Rinpoche (Tib. stag-sna-rin-pa-che)

Tagna Rinpoche was born in Tibet. He got his early education under the guidance of Jamgon Nawang Gyaltsen[4]. In 1695 he arrived Lhasa offered prayer in the famous temple of 'Jo Sakyamuni' then went to Chos-zong gon temple[5]. After sometime he got invitation from king Nima Namgyal[6] to visit Ladakh.

Therefore, he arrived in Ladakh, later with the kind support of king he constructed Tagna monastery near Ladakh. Sonam Lundup[7], the Prime Minister of Ladakh also helped him in this religious works. In 1711, Rinpoche returned Tibet and spent maximum time in Dugdan[8] and Kham[9] areas till his last breath.

First Incarnation

Karma Stanzin[10] was the first incarnation of Stagna Rinpoche. He was born in Tibet, received his primary education from the concerned monastery. He arrived in Zanskar via Kham, Cho Padma[11], Garza[12] etc. Under the guidance of famous lama Zodpa he worked for the Zongkhu monastery[13].

Second Incarnation

The second incarnation Tashi stanphel[14] was born in Markha valley[15]. He got initial education at his monastery in Ladakh, later went to Dug-dan for higher education in Buddhism under Drugpa K'agyug tradition[16]. He studied Buddhist Philosophy and logic from the important monasteries in Tibet. After coming in Ladakh he devoted himself for the development of monastic activities. He involved in the welfare works and against the Begari system. In those days under this system every family of a village according to turn had to provide their services to state Government officers in free of cost. Besides, they had to supply ponies and carried their loads from one stage to another, even monasteries were not being exempted, Lamas of the concerned, welcomed them and ready at their services at various stages on way between srinagar and leh route. Tagna Rinpoche raised voice against this system, and asked Maharaja Gulab Singh to exempt monasteries from Begari rule. He offered a precious stone 'Nilam' to Maharaja Gulab Singh in this connection.

Third Incarnation

He was born in Spituk village[17] and got early education in the monastery, later went to Tibet for higher education in Buddhist Philosophy. However, didn't return and passed away in Tibet.

Present Incarnation

He was born in Marshilang (Tib. Martselang)[18] in 1920. His father Padma Dadul and mother Rigzin Wangmo belonged to poor family. When stag-tsang rinpoche of Hemis monastery got this information, he requested his parents to bring him to Hemis monastery for further look after. He brought to Hemis monastery where stag-tsang rinpoche performed special rituals and named him Nawang Toldan. He got basic education in Drug-pa k'agyud monasteries in Ladakh, later devoted himself wholeheartedly in religious works. Under his leadership Leh Zo-Khang was constructed. He visited Zanskar several times and repaired Bardan and Sani monasteries. At present stays in leh.

Devang gyatso (Tib.de dvang rgya mtso)

He was a famous lama of Zanskar during 16th century. He was born in a royal family in Padum[19], got early education under the umbrella of Drugpa Ka'gyul tradition. Later practiced meditation and became Siddha. People believe that he was the incarnation of Sari Putra.[20]

In the middle of 16th century he visited Thar-la, to see the ruins of Bardan gonpa, he made up his mind to reconstruct this. Accordingly, the monastery was constructed and he gave new name ' Bar dan sangyas chos ling'.

It is said that when the construction work of the above monastery was going on, some evil spirits created obstruction, as a result he was bound to stop this auspicious work for several times. In those days stag-tsang Respa[21] was in Zanskar, he requested him to purify the site and remove the evil spirits from the construction site. On his request stag-tsang Respa by his spiritual power stopped the nonsense activities of evil spirits. Bardan monastery was finally constructed. Stag-tsang Respa stayed one month there, thereafter returned to Zungkhul, then went his long journey for Uddyana.[22]

Devang gyatso later developed Bardan monastery under Drug pa K'agyud tradition. He visited extensively throughout in

Zanskar as well as Lahul-Spiti and propagated his tradition. In his last days he stayed in *sha-shur* monastery[23], Keylong[24], the same later came under the administrative control of Bardan monastery. After his perinirvana some more monasteries of Lahul e.g. Tupciling, Gurughantal etc. started function under the direction of Bardan monastery. Today to fulfil the needs of these monasteries, Bardan monastery sent two lamas as *pujari*. This tradition is still preserved.

Sras Rinpoche (Tib. Cang tse chorje sras sbul rin po che)

Rinpoche was born in 1824. After joining Bhikshu Sangha he was named 'Sras Rinpoche'. Later studied Buddhist Philosophy under the Gelukpa tradition, unfortunately didn't live long and passed away at the age of 39 years. His incarnation Tsulthim chosphel[25] was born in 1864 in Yang thang family. His father Sonam Stanzin[26] and mother Jorzom were true Buddhists, therefore, donated him to the monastery. Under Tsulthim Dorje[27] he studied Buddhist Philosophy and literature, then went to Tibet for further studies. In Tibet he studied Bodth Vidhyas under the guidance of learned lamas popular among them was lama Lobzang Tsulthim gyatso. He visited Kahm, Pashod[28] etc. in Tibet, finally returned Rizong monastery[29], brought many Buddhist Pothis, which are still preserved in the monastery. In his last days he preached neighouring villagers, e.g., Saspol, Hemishukpachan etc. At the age of 63, he got parinirvana. The present Sras Rinpoche Stanzin Norbu was born in Matho village in 1928[30]. He became lama of Rizong monastery. Thereafter offered Rinpoche Throne. Stok khanpo (Omachikpa) gave him primary education, he went to *Dras pung dan sa*[31] monastery in Tibet for higher studies and got highest degree in Buddhist Philosophy 'Lharampa'. On the request of Rizong lamas and Ladakhis returned Ladakh. He is a learned scholar rinpoche of Ladakh and at present holds the highest honourable post of Geluk pa tradition '*cang tse chos je*'.[32]

Notes and References

1. Nawang Tsering : 'rig p'ai bdud rtsi', C.I.B.S. (nd.):13.

2. *Ibid*: 15-16.

3. *Ibid*:16.

4. Jamgon Nawang Gyaltsen : Tib. 'ajam mgon nag dbang rgyal mtshen.

5. Chos-zong-gon: Tib. Chos dzong dgon.

6. Nima Namgyal : He was the son of king Delegs Namgyal. He ruled Ladakh 1680-1780. During his reign Jesuit Desideri came Leh in 1715 on his way to Lhasa. He married twice. His first wife died after the birth of Deskyong Namgyal. Zizi Khatun of Purig was his second wife. King had two issues from her Trashi Namgyal and Trashi Wangmo. Cf. Francke, A.H.: 'A History of Western Tibet; Asian ed. Services, New Delhi; 1995 (Reprinted) : 115-119.

7. Kalon Sonam Lundup : Tib. bk'a blon bsod nams lhun grup. He was the Prime Minister in the King Nima Namgyal regime.

8. Dugdan : Tib. 'abrug gdan.

9. Kham : Tib. Khams (Pron. Kham). It is under Chinese provine of Sichuan. From Dartsedo two ancient trade routes diverge, the Ayalam and the Janglam, the former going all the way through to Ladakh, the latter to Kashger. Cf. Finegan, Jack: 'Tibet: A Dreamt of Image', Tibet House; New Delhi; 1986: 1-2.

10. Karma Stanzin : Tib. Karma bstan 'adzin.

11. Cho-Padma ; mtsho –padma.

12. Garza : Lahul (Himachal Pradesh state).

13. Zongkhul monastery : It lies on the Padum – Kishtwar trekking route, just before the ascent to Oma-ri la begins, and situated in a swallow's nest on the rock face of the Ating gorge.

14. Tashi Stanphel: Tib. bkra shi bstan 'aphel.

15. Markha valley :
Lat. 33° 51'
Long. 77° 25'

This village is situated on the right bank of the river of the same name, 10 miles above Nemo. It is passed on the route from Padum to Leh via the Riberang pass. Cf. Gazetteer of Kashmir and Ladak-vivek Pub. 1974 (Reprinted): 590.

16. Drug-pa k'agyud tradition ; Tib.'brug pa (Pron. Druk-pa) suborder of the k'agyud-pa tradition. It was founded by gling ras pa pad ma rdo rje (Pron. ling repa Pema dorje) during twelve century. In about 1180 his disciple Tsangpo Gya re pa founded the main monastery Relung, 48 km southeast of Gyangze and the monastery 'drug (Pron. Druk), 64 km southwest of Lhasa, later from this monastery drug-pa sect came into existence stag-tsang res pa took the responsibility to spread Drug-pa teaching in the Western Tibet from his guru Lha rtse ba nagwang zang po. It was through his efforts that Drugpa-order gained its great prominence in Ladakh. Cf. Finegan Jack; *op.cit.*: 97-98.

17. Spituk village : Tib. Spi-thug.
Lat. 34° 10'
Long. 77° 35'
Elev. 10,700 feet.

It is located on the right bank of the Indus River, 5 miles south-west of Leh and near Kushok Bakula Airport. Cf. Gazetteer of Kashmir and Ladakh: 66.

18. Martselang : Tib. mar rtse lang
Lat. 33° 50'
Long. 77° 45'
Elev. 12,200 feet

It is located on the left bank of the Indus River, about 22 miles away from Leh. Gazetteer; *op.cit.*: 590.

19. Padum : It is the only town in Zanskar (Tib. Zangskar) Tashil in Kargil district of Ladakh.

20. Sari Putra: He was the main disciple of Sakyamuni Buddha.

21. Stag-tsang raspo: Paksam Wangpo was invited to Ladakh by king Jamyang Namgyal, but he didn't come. Later stag-tsang raspa came in Ladakh and propagated Drug-pa tradition.

22. Uddiyana : Urgyan (Pron. Urgyan), which was the Sanskrit Uddiyana, ancient Swat, then under the rule of the blind king Indrabhuti, Cf. Finegan, Jack; *op.cit.*: 50.

23. Sha-shur monastery : It is located at the north of Keylong;

Lahul-Spiti district, H.P. Devang gyatso clay statue is in this monastery in which his relics are placed.

24. Keylong : It is the district headquarter of Lahul-spiti district of Himachal Pradesh state.

25. Tsultim Chosphel : Tib. Tshul khrims chos' aphel.

26. Sonam Stanzin : Tib. bstod nams bstan 'adzin.

27. Tsulthim Dorje : Tib. Tshul-tim rdo rje.

28. Pashod: Tib.dp'a shod.

29. Rizong monastery : Tib. ri dzong monastery. This monastery was founded by Tsulthim Nima during the beginning of 19th century.

30. Sonam Phuntsog; Ladakh, 2000:77-78.

31. Dras pung dan sa : Tib. 'abras sbungs gden sa.

32. Cang tse chos je: Tib. byang rtse chos rje; the highest honourable post in post in Geluk pa order after Tsong-khapa.

13

Some Important Lamas Attached to Deskit Monastery

Panchen Lama (Nubrapa)

Panchen Lama was born at Udmaru village in Nubra valley. At childhood named Lobzang Stanba. He studied some Buddhist texts in the nearby monastery under the guidance of a lama. Later, went to Tashiluunpo monastery in Tibet for further study. He studied Buddhist logic and Philosophy under the guidance of Lama Jamyang Lobzang of Thosam Ling. Then became Khanpo of Kilkhang Tasang. He decorated the temple by various Buddhist statues, wall paintings and installed one of the popular statue of Gyalva Gendundup (Panchen lama) in the temple. Gradually, became popular among Buddhist society in Tibet and was known as Lama Buston Rinchen Dup. Thereafter became the head lama of Jalung-gon. He spent most of his time in preaching. Moreover, didn't forget his native land and country, so returned to Nubra. He stayed in Deskit monastery, brought many religious things from Tibet and donated the same to Deskit monastery. Soonafter, he preached villagers of Nubra valley as well as lamas of the surrounding monasteries. Many of them became his disciples. Janyang Santipa, Lotos Gyaltsen etc.were of his popular disciples in Ladakh. During Hor invasion he was killed. His body is still preserved in chorten at Carasa Lhakhang. Here follows an interesting storey about his killing.

"When Hor invaded Ladakh a Horpa soldier cut down Panchen lama head and threw his body into the river. Surprisingly his head flew into the sky and went to Tayagar village, where it hanged through a tree. The other parts of his body floated to Deskit. At the bank of river villagers at Deskit endeavoured to pull the body, it was too heavy to carry. So, they again threw it into the water. Later the same reached at the river bank near Carasa village. When the villagers saw this, they pulled out the body from the river. Here it became so light that they easily carried to the Carsa temple, where lamas performed rituals and placed the same in the chorten, which is still preserved in the temple. Because, gold had been used for making the above chorten, therefore, popularly known 'Serdun chorten'.

Choje Spon Paljor

He was the head lama of Thiksey monastery. During King Tsewang Stanba visited Nubra valley. He retreated near the Deskit monastery and attained spiritual power by the blessing of a lha, later decided to build a chuglakhang in the monastery. Then the king and queen of Nubra sponsored for this auspicious work. He made Buddha statue with the help of local artists. Within a short time, built another temple and placed Tsong-khapa statue. For the welfare of lamas of Deskit monastery he gave gonpa land to villagers on rent. Gradually, he decorated temples by Buddhist painting. This time he didn't forget to make king Tsewang and Tundup gyalmo paintings on the wall as they sponsored to build the temple.

Chosje Palgyaltsan

He belonged to Cacang family and was born in Deskit. He was a honest and characterful person. When he was only 5 years old got admission in a nearby gonpa, went to Tibet for further education. In Tibet he took admission in Tashilunpo monastery.

Here, studied Pharcin, Jot, Dulva, Namdel etc. Thereafter became Khanpo of Kilkhang. He taught Tashilumpo students, later returned to Nubra and stayed in Deskit monastery, named 'ca-cangpe'. He didn't sit idle, started to give teachings to lamas and villagers. One of his followers made his statue while he was alive and later placed in the Deskit monastery.

Kachen Lozang Condos

He was born in Nubra. At the age of five years took admission in Deskit monastery as lama. He studied basic ritual things and learned Bodhi grammar under the guidance of senior lamas. At the of 15years went to Tibet for further higher studies in Philosophy and Buddhist logic.

14

Nawang Tsering (Tib. dga dbang tse ring) : A great Buddhist Scholar of Zanskar

Dub chen Nawang Tsering[1] was born in Zanskar at Ating[2] on 14th September 1657[3]. He got early education under the guidance of learned lamas in the concerned monastery. Meme Kungga was his main teacher.

Nawang Tsering had especial attachment with Bardan monastery. He studied various Buddhist texts under the guidance of Dug-pa ka' gyud[4] lamas of the monastery. After strengthening Dug-pa tradition of Mahayana Buddhism in Zanskar he visited Lahul and Spiti regions for the propagation of Buddhism. In Lahul[5] and Monyul[6] he meditated for some time, later gave preaching to people. He renovated some old Lhakhangs in Lahul and re-established Dug-pa ka'gyud order. Thereafter he founded Buddha Sangha in his respective monasteries. He trained a few lamas according to Ka'gyud monastic tradition, later returned to Zon-khul[7].

In 1684, he decided to build Zon-khul monastery under Dug-pa tradition. After the completion of various temples in this monastery he installed various Buddhis statues, some of them stated below.[8]

1. Dorje Chang (Tib. rdo-rje tsang)

2. Thub-vang (Tib. Thub-dbang)

3. Sakyamuni Buddha (Tib. sangs rab bdum)

4. Orgyan-tso-khor (Tib. 'ao rgyan gtsor sogs bzhengs).

According to 'kaya', 'vaka' and 'chitta' of Buddhist tradition he brought some important Buddhist texts. Some of them written by golden ink. Popular among them are:[9]

1. Lama Nam thar (Tib. bla ma rnam thar)

2. Urgyan Padma Nam thar.

The Zongkhul is famous as cave monastery in Ladakh. It is associated with famous Indian Yogis, such as Naropa. The caves around which the present establishment had been developed by Lama Nawang Tsering being used by the famous lamas and yogis for solitary meditation. Before the propagation of Buddhism in Zanskar and Lahul and Spiti regions he too retreated at the above caves for some time.

In order to get faith of Zanskar people he arranged to celebrate Annual feast featival every year on 4th month of the Tibetan calendar in Zon-khul monastery. Gradually devotees from far and wide of Zanskar sarted to visit the above monastery and attend the annual festival.

In conclusion Nawang Tsering was a great Buddhist saint of his time he propagated Dug pa ka' gyud tradition in Zanskar and Lahul and Spiti region. In 1731, he passed away at the age of 74 years.

Notes and References

1. Dub Chen Nawang Tsering: Tib. grub chen ngga dbang tse ring. He was a great Buddhist yogi of Zanskar.

2. Ating: It is a Buddhists dominated villages in Zanskar of Kargil district. The Zong-khol cave monastery is situated on a rock facing the Ating gorge.

3. Sonam Phuntsog: Ladakh, 2000 : 57.

4. Dug pa ka' gyud : Tib. 'abrug pa bka' brgyud.

5. Lahul : Tib. gar-zha: It is with Spiti region known Lahul-Spiti district of Himachal Pradesh. It is said that during 17th century it was under Ladakh kingdom and all the religious activities were governed by either Zanskar monasteries or by Hemis.

6. Monyul : Tib. mon-yul.

7. Zon-khul: Tib. rdzong khul. It falls on the Padum-Kishtwar trekking route.

8. Sonam Phuntsog; op.cit.: 57.

9. *Ibid.*

15

Tsering Skarma : A Famous Sculptor of Ladakh

It is said that under Buddhist Art tradition Buddha statue was made during the life-time of Buddha by Indra with the help of Visvakarma. Later Buddha himself consecrated the statue when it was completed. Thereafter on the request of king of China Spritimjaya Dharmapala sent him Jowo statue.

In seventh century King Tsong-tsan Gampo got married with Konajo, the princess of Chinese king Thai-Manju. The king offered him the statue of Jowo as a wedding gift. Then king built a temple for Jowo and installed it there. Gradually this art spread in Ladakh via Kashmir, when Lotsava Rinchen Zangpo with the help of thirty two Kashmiri artists constructed 108 Lhakhang and chortens in West Tibet including Ladakh. Infact the present sculpture art tradition flourish during and after 15th century.

On 28th October 2006, I got an invitation from Tsering Skarma, a famous 'spon' (or artist) of Ladakh, for a lunch at his residence on 29th i.e. Sunday. It was a good opportunity for me to ask something on Ladakhi art. Next day about 10 A.M. I went to Lama Standar residence and requested him to join me lunch at

Tsering Skarma's residence. He readily accepted my request. About 11 o'clock we reached his residence at Agling, Leh-Ladakh. Tsering Skarma was not in his residence, his two disciples were busy in making statues. I asked :

"Where is Tsering Skarma's residence?"

"To follow this street, at the end you'll find two storeyed building, climb to glass room through stairs, you'll find him there."

We followed the same and went into the glass room.

"Julley, Gyen le!" Tsering Skarma welcomed us.

" He is Dr. Prem Singh Jina, eminent scholar and writer, my teacher." Lama Standar introduced me with Tsering Skarma.

"Oh, Julley; you are welcome please be seated."

"Thanks."

After some time he asked his daughter to bring tea for us. She did the same. I didn't take tea, Ladakhi tea biscuits etc. Therefore, he asked his daughter to bring a glass of milk for me. After taking one or two sip I asked.

" Aa ba le, did you heard my name before?"

" Yes, Padmashi Tsering Wangdus Thanka Painter told me about you."

"O.K. Please give me your brief introduction."

"I was born on 28th August 1938 in Hemishukpacan village. My father Phunchok Rabgyal and Mother Diskit later sent me to Khalatse to learn Thanka painting under the guideance of famous artist Tsewang Rigzin[1]. I belongs to a poor family, thereafter, Sonam Norbu Ralkapa took my full responsibily and bore all my expenses".

"Can you tell me a few words about your teacher Rev. Tsewang Rigzin.

"My Guru Rev. Tsewang Rigzin was one of the most famous sculptors of his time. He belongs to Lingshet village, later came to Khalatse. He was not only famous in Ladakh, even in Tibet. The abbot of Tholing monastery in Tibet invited him to build Yamantaka statue[2]. On the completion of this statue, the abbot remarked, 'such master piece of work is alone a example of Tibetan art in entire Tibet.' Under such great artist I learnt Thanka painting for nine years. Later under his supervision started to make Thankas for thirty six years. Thereafter started to make Buddhist statues. My teacher Rev. Tsewang Rigzing died in 1970. It was a great loss to Ladakh and to the Nation."

"In which style do you make thanka?".

"My style of Thanka painting is known Can-dis[3] tradition. In my painting you'll find brown colour background. Besides there are many other style of thanka paintings e.g. Udis[4], Kham dis[5] etc."

"In your opinion which style of Thanka painting is the oldest?"

"Probably Kham dis. In my opinion this tradition flourished in Tibet during 10th century. It has Chinese art influence. My teacher Rev. Tsewang Rigzin also used this style of painting under this tradition like Chinese art light stone colours are used while making thanka or wall paintings. His Holiness 14th Dalai lama also like this painting."

"Can you tell me how this tradition came in Kham from China?"

"According to Tibetan Chronicle before 10th century there was a famous Tibetan artist named Samunda Tundup. He was in his previous incarnation born in China, and was the incarnation of Manjusri. In Tibet, during 10th century when he was born at first learned Tibetan grammar, but soon got married. He had not good relations with his wife, took divorce and came to Kham. On his way to Kham he found *Pardong* (a box)[6]. He thought it would be a good sign, carried this *Pardong*, he arrvied near Kham and again found a 'chart' for the biginners of Thanka painting. He now decided that he should learn Thanka painting. He put the Thanka painting chart in *Pardong* and moved ahead. Now he started seaching Thanka painting teacher. At Yasdok Staglung[7] village he asked from villagers about Painting teacher. Some one told him there was one painting teacher in his village, named Tashi Gyalpo[8]. According he searched Tashi Gyalpo and requested to teach him how to make Thanka painting? Later learned Painting and became more popular than his teacher. Once he saw a Chinese Thanka in Tibet. It was of *Sithang Gyajat Chenpo*[9], immediately his mind struck as if it was made by him; might be in his previous incarnation. Later for the benefit of his fellow students he wrote a book on Thanka painting."

" How many Thankas you have made?"

"I have made many Thankas, here follows some of them (Table : 15:1).

Table 15.1: Thankas made by Spon Skarma

Name of Thanka	*Name of gonpo/place for whom thanka was made*	*Height/year*
Sakya Thuba	Khalatse (1st thanka)	-
Samanla Desegyat	Hemis Gonpa	-
Guru Tsangyat	Hemis Gonpa	1976
16 Arhats	Hemis Gonpa	1976
Tuskhor	Hemis Gonpa	1976
Dechok	Hemis Gonpa	1976
Tandin	Hemis Gonpa	1976

(All the above thankas were made during the period of Belo Rinpoche, Chagzot of Hemis Gonpa and under the director of Hemis Welfare Society.)

"Did you make wall paintings?"

"Yes, not many, in Phungchokling monastery at Hemishukpacan I made 16 Arhts."

"When did you start to make Buddhist Statues?"

"I started to make Buddhist Statues bit late. At the age of 66 years Rev. Tsewang Rigzin suggested me to start to make statues as I was very old and could not make the same."

"You are a famous painter and sculptor, why didn't you apply for the post of Lecturer in Painting or Master Craftman in Central Institute of Buddhist Studies, Leh?"

"During eighties (80's) I was called for an interview for the post of instructor in Handicraft Center. J&K State Govt. My two collegues and disciples of Rev. Tsewang Rigzin named Nawang Tsering and Sonam Skalzang were also called for the same post. I thought I should not go, as I couldn't do justice for my students if I would have government post and might be busy in statues making, may be in the coming future this Tibetan statue making tradition disappear from Ladakh. Therefore, for the welfare of my students and for the preservation or protection of this art and culture I decided to remain at home and continue to give training to my students about statue making privately. In this way I may pay more attention than those sculptors who are in government jobs."

"Is there any difference between the measuring units of Thanka painting and statue making?"

"According to Tibetan tradition for making Buddhist statues every artist will have to learn Thanka painting. In Thanka painting artists use two kinds of measuring units viz, Tuskyi khorlo and Dum zung Khorlo. While in statue making the following units are used :

1.	Tho	All are the same measuring units and in general called 'Bur'.
2.	Thil	
3.	Thamlo	
4.	Chasen	
5.	Sdong	

For example – The measurement between forehead and chin =12 sor and one Sor = one angul.

For measuring the depth of the statue the following units are used-

Sor	All has the same meaning
Chaung	
Chatang	

"How many statues have you made?"

"I have many small and medium statues for public and for the Buddhist monasteries. Here follows some of them (Table 15.2)".

Table : 15.2 Buddhist Statues made by Spon Skarma Tsering

S.No.	*Name of the Statue*	*Place/Gonpo where Statue is placed*	*Height (feet)*
1.	Maitreya[10] (Took three years, in each year did three months work during summer)	Lingshet Gonpa	27

(Contd.)

(Contd.)

S.No.	Name of the Statue	Place/Gonpo where Statue is placed	Height (feet)
2.	Co-Rinpoche (1984-85)	Lhakhang Soma in Hemishukpacan	27
3.	Dukar (Three faces and 6 hands)	Skampo do Lhakhang in Skampo do (Rev. Tsewang Rigzin was then one of the member of Hemis Welfare Committee)	5'
4.	Apchi Choskyi Dolma	Yuru monastery in Gonkhang (1968, his teacher also helped him)	4
5.	Rigsumgonpo	Yurukhang Onpo Khanpa (1969-70)	5
6.	Rigsumgonpo	Skangchang Khanpa (1969-70)	Ava-5 Others 3
7.	Rigsumgonpo	Sonam Phelpa; Khalatse	-do-
8.	Kunkhen Padma karpo	Muth Gonpa Stagna Gonpa	10 10
9.	Guru Rinpoche		
10.	Carok Doncan Gonpo Chagzee Paldan Lhamo Namsras Gonkar Tsemara	called Choskyong (1983-84)	2-3 2-3 2-3 2-3 2-3 2-3

(Contd.)

(Contd.)

S.No.	*Name of the Statue*	*Place/Gonpo where Statue is placed*	*Height (feet)*
11.	Skyova Jigsten Gonpo (yabsras sum)	Shacukul Gonpa	20-2
12.	Buddha	Gonkhang of	9
	Dechok	Shacukul	-
	Tsemara	Gonpa	-
	Apchi Choskyi Dolma	-	
	Gonpo Chagzee		-
	Lama Dorje chang		-
13.	Chamba	Tharuk (in Chang Thang)	19
14.	Sangyas Opakmet		7
	Guru Rinpoche	Chushul	7
	Sangyas 4 hands	Gonpa	7
	Avaloktesvara ⎤	(1998)	6
	Skyopa ⎦	2000	6
15.	Avalokitesvara-One thousand hands	Aerat Near Chushul	7
16.	-do-	Sman merak (Phobrang)	7
17.	Sangyas	Phobrang Lhakhang Yogma	10
18.	-do-	Pholonglas (Chang Thang)	10

(Contd.)

(Contd.)

S.No.	*Name of the Statue*	*Place/Gonpo where Statue is placed*	*Height (feet)*
19.	Tsongkhapa Yabsras Sum	Stongde Gonpa	Main 27 Others 16 each
20.	Buddha	-do-	10
21.	Sangyas cokor sum Buddha + Sari & Mon	Tsandar Gonpa	4 3 and 3
22.	Sangyas marmezat	-do-	4
23.	Sakyathuba	-do-	4
24.	Camba Rinpoche	-do-	4
25.	Padmasambhava	Nemo (Drugpa ka' gyud Gonpa)	10
26.	Maitreya	Likir	70
27.	Co-Rinpoche	-do-	5
28.	Padmasambhava	-do-	5
29.	14th Dalai Lama (Avalokitesvara)	Zive Tsal Photang (Soma)	7
30.	Kanlop Cokorsum (Padmasambhava+ Khato Budhisattva + Chorgyal Thetug Decan)	–do-	Main 1 Others 6" each

(Contd.)

(Contd.)

S.No.	*Name of the Statue*	*Place/Gonpo where Statue is placed*	*Height (feet)*
31.	Geva Yabsras Sum (Tsungkhapa+Khadupje +Gyalshabje)	-do-	-do-
32.	Maitreya (Under Construction)	Diskit Gonpa	90'
33.	Padmasambhava	Under –do- construction	5'
34.	Buddha		5'
35.	Tsongkhapa		5'
36.	Padmasmbhava	Ranbhirpura	5'
37.	-do-	Tangtse Manskhang	6'
38.	Kunkhen Padma karpo	-do-	7'
39.	Buddha	Ladakh Scout	6'
40.	Padmasambhava	-do-(karu)	5'

To sum up I would say Tsering Skarma[11] is a good sculptor of our age and has developed a passion for this art from a very young age. He belongs to the remote village in Shyam side of Ladakh. With the passage of time he has made hundreds statues adoring Buddhist houses and monasteries of Ladakh. Therefore, his work and this art tradition being appreciated all over Ladakh (Appendix 15.1, 15.2 and 15.3).

Notes and References

1. Tsewang Rigzin : He was born in Linghet village. His teacher Gongspon was also from Lingshet. He after taking early education

in Lingshet gonpa went to Tashilunpo monastery for further study. In Tashilunpo monastery he took the training for making Thanka painting, statue making etc. Later returned to Lingshet, but didn't stay there and came to Khalatse.

2. Yamantaka statue : He is the frecious form and manifestation of Manjusri.

3. Can-dis : Tib. gcan bris.

4. Udis : Tib. dbu bris.

5. Kham-dis : Tib. kham bris

6. Pardong : It is a box in which Tibetan painters put their painting items.

7. Yasdok Staglung : Tib. gyas grog stag klung.

8. Tashi Gyalpo.

9. Sithang Gyajat Chenpo : Tib. Si thang ya bjo chen po.

10. Maitreya = Future Buddha: Rev. Tsewang Rigzin was the great painter of his time and belongs to Lingshet village. But didn't make any painting and Buddhist statue for Lingshet monastery. Therefore, Lingshet villagers and Lingshet gonpa welfare society invited Rev. Tsewang Rigzin's student Skarma Tsering to make Maitreya statue as a sign of Rev. Tsewang Rigzin artistic work. Accordingly Skarma visited Lingshet gonpa. He asked Lingshet sculptors to make head and hands of the Maitreya and rest of the part he would himself make. But Lingshet sculptors couldn't do so and went to Zanskar. Later Skarma completed the whole Maitreya statue alone.

11. Skarma Tsering : At present he has some outstanding students as cited below:
    1. Tsering Paljor from Tia village.
    2. Norbu of Matho village.

3. Sonam Dorje of Chushul village.
4. Rev. Konchok Thabdol of Tar village.
5. Jigmet Wangchok of Hemishukpacan.

APPENDIX-15.1

la dvag klu dgon dg'a ldan dar rgyas glang likir Monastery Ladakh.

Certificate

I, the undersigned hereby certify that Skarma Tsering is a expert sculptor, has built 72 feet statue of Maitreya.

I, further giving this certificate with some gifts on behalf of Likir lamas and head lamas of the monastery on 16th cow year of 14th of 7th month.

Sd

Thijin Lozang Tharcin

APPENIX-15.2
Sculpture Art Lineage in Ladakh

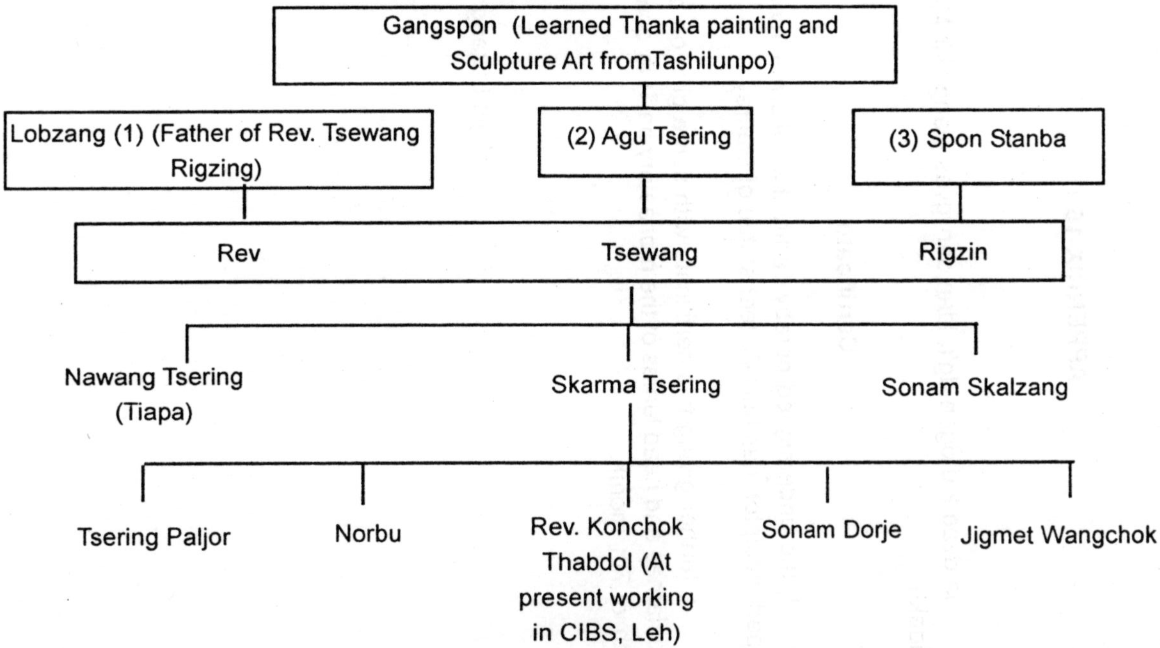

APPENDIX – 15.3

Life and works of Rev. Konchok Thapdol

Name : Rev. Konchok Thapdol

Father's Name : Skalzang Phunchok

Mother's Name : Sonam Palkit

Buddhist Sculptures made by Rev. Konchok Thapdol.

S. No.	*Name of Statue*	*Place/gonpa*	*Height (feet)*
1.	Co-Rinpoche	Lamayuru gonpa	07
2.	Skyova Rinpoche	"	03
3.	Maitreya	"	
4.	Skyova Jigsten	(Chamra)	03
5.	Buddha	Yulang (Zanskar)	12
6.	Tsongkhapa	Camsen (Nubra)	10
7.	Maitreya	"	12
8.	Padmasambhava (Khansum Zilnon)	Skhampuk gonpa	08
9.	Stay Tsang Shamo Natho	"	05
10.	Kunkhen Padma Karpo	"	05

(Contd.)

(Contd.)

S. No.	*Name of Statue*	*Place/gonpa*	*Height (feet)*
11.	Paldan Lhamo	"	04
12.	Khanglop chos sum	Angle (Anley Tashi Chosling Gonpa)	5-08
13.	Dubchan Thangston Gyalpo	"	03
14.	Guru Dorje Dolot	"	03
15.	Guru Rinpoche	Chumathang Gonpa	31/2
16.	Canpo Gyara	"	3
17.	Kunkhen Padma Karpo	"	3
18.	Avalokitesvara (1000 hands)	"	4
19.	Co-Rinpoche	"	3
20.	Apchi Chosdon	Ladok Tangtse monastery	3
21.	Gonpo 4-hands	"	4
22.	Choskyong Tsemara	"	3.5
23.	Buddha with Sari and Mod	Tangtse (To-To Gonpa)	3-5
24.	Ka'gyut Ser-thing (Aleven small Statues)	Shacukul monastery	11/2
25.	Apchi Choskyi Dolma	Durbuk monastery	3
26.	Skyova Digsten Gonpo	Shyok Lhakhang	3.5
27.	Apchi Choskyi Dolma	"	3.5
28.	Sangyas Opakmet	Choglamsar Karmapa Gonpa	10
29.	Avalokitesvara with one thousand hands	"	05

(Contd.)

(Contd.)

S. No.	*Name of State*	*Place/gonpa*	*Height (feet)*
30.	Lama Dorje Chang	"	5
31.	Padmasambhava	"	5
32.	Padmasambhava	"	5
33.	Padmasambhava	Choglamsar Village Gonpa	4
34.	Padmasambhava	Lhe Tsokhang	10
35.	Guru Dushet	Timasgang Mane Lhakhang	11
36.	Padmasambhava (Guru Khamsum Jilnon)	Urgyan Dorje Choszong (Near Sabu Village)	8
37.	Buddha	"	5
38.	Dregung Skyova Rinpoche	"	5
39.	Duzong Rinpoche	"	5
40.	Buddha	Koyul monastery (Leh-skara)	11
41.	Avalokitesvara with one thousand hands	sNenas Khang	8

16

A Tibetan Manuscript During King Tsetan Namgyal Period

Tsetan Namgyal was the king of Ladakh during the beginning of 19th century. Though he didn't sponsore much for the construction of Buddhist monasteries in Ladakh, inclined towards Buddhism and constructed a big Mani wall near Radio Station, Leh. It consists Mani Mantra viz. as 'Om Mani Padma Hum'. This is Arya Avalokitesvara mantra. On the surface of Mani wall lakhs Mani mantras engraved on stones or flat stones. It is not necessary to engrave whole Avalokitesvara mantra on each stone. Normally, each word of the above mantra is engraved e.g. Om, Mani, Padme and Hum.

Tsentan Namgyal constructed above Mani wall as well as on its ends cang-cub chortens. The surface of the Mani wall covered by about 10 lakh engraved Mani mantra slates.

Sonam Lhundup Omacik pa of Stok village was great Buddhist scholar. Tsetan Namgyal when came to know about his Buddhist knowledge and literature, decided to give him the responsibility to correct all engraved Mani mantras. It was a difficult task to correct around 10 lakh engraved mantras. He didn't bother and wholeheartedly devoted himself for correcting the said Arya Avalokitesvara mantras.

The mani wall are constructed for the welfare of human beings. All mani walls have various mani mantras. Therefore, Buddhists and all people who have religious faith on Buddhism, walk at the right side of the above monument to get puniya.

The above auspicious work when successfully completed by Sonam Lhundup Omacik pa, King Tsetan Namgyal very much pleased and order his ministers to give him all facilities as their ministers enjoyed. Thus he was given 27 canals land in Stok village, exempted from 'Bari' or 'Begari' system underwhich each household had to work for his Majesty officials in free of cost. He was also allowed to provide fuel wood in free of cost.

Tibetan Text in Classical Language and Orthography

Yangs p'ai nor 'adzing khyon la stohs thugs gse gyi 'akhor los bsgyur ba bstan 'adzin chos kyi rgyal po Tse brtan rnam rgyal rdo rje mi 'argyud dbag gi sdo 'ai gk'a dang yabsu gtogs p'a skye rgu yang skya mchog dman sbyi dang bye brag dog mkar dpon blon po gnyer pa grong dpon do ga che chibas dpon bya ba zhi dragi don la mngags p'ai skyu tshab las kyi sno mod togs so tsog la springs pa mi'ai dbang po 'abod pa dge ldan bse kuns blangs te lha dang bcas p'ai 'gro ba yongs kyi mchod sdong chyogs las rnam par rgyal b'ai thugs. Sten rnam ghis dang 'aphags mchog spyan ras gzigs kyi yang shing yi ge drug ma 'abum ther 'ace mo'ai grangs ldar sgrubs pa 'ai skabs su 'ao ma gcig sa bsod names bsdan 'adzin 'ade yas' aphags yul gyi yi ge........... yig drug brid dang yig bris pa dang rto brkos pa bcas skyi zhus zhus dag bsko bzhag byas par khongs kyad mi dbang bdgi bk'a spyi por bcidas du rgya gar gyi yi ge bri ba dang zhus dag sog 'agran zla bral ba 'adi gar dgongs par 'abyor b'ai bstan don gyi zhabs 'adogs khungs ltar grub b'ai kyud la brtan togs shi nas rin mang bred ba rca stong mkhar gyis khungs yin p'ai 'asros rin mang zer p'ai kra ku gdo 'aog ghyis gsod names bstan 'adzing gyi bu rgyud bcas par kang sar bk'a drin skyags pa yin p'ai gong khod kyi las snor rtogs rigs drag zhan nth'a dag nas char pa chu grogs kyi phan grogs byed pas las gnod 'atho bsam sbyor ngan p'ai khral regs 'agel ba dang za rgyud du snyad p'ai glong ngan su'ai thad byas pa shar tshe byed pa po 'ai lus steng du khrips kyi zhes gnon gtong des nyin pas de ltar mi dgos p'ai phyag rgy' ai 'a bru don tsad mar bzung b'ai skal ba ze srid bar kharal rigsu rgyud pa spu tsam yang med pad bde bar gnas cug pa gal che che.........lcags spro zla yar tses mchog rdu dge bar yo brong sle mkhar rtse nar bris..

Text in Roman Transliteration

Yang pe nor zin khyon la stop thug ser gyi khor lo gyur va stan zin chos kyi gyal po Tse ten namgyal doje mi gyur vang gi doi ka dang jab su tog pa kye gu yang kya chog man ci dang ce dag tog khar pon lon po nyer pa dong on toga che chibas pon ca va ji tagi don la ngags pe ku tsab las kyi no mor togs so cog la tings pa mi vang por bod pa ge dan se kan langs te la dang cas pe do va yongs kyi chot dong chogs la nam par gyal ve thugs ten nam nyis dang phag thog can ras zigs kyi yang nying yi go dug me bum ther ce mot dang dar dubs pe kabs su oma cig sa sod nam tan zin di yas phags yul gyi yi ge ....yig dug ti va dang yig di pa dang to kas pas cas kyi ju tag ko jag cas par khong kyang mi vang gi ka ci por cids du gya gar gyi yi ge di va dang jus dag sog dan la dal va di gar gongs par jor ve stan don gyi jabs dogs khungs tar dub pe kyud la ten togs shi nas rin mang zer ve ca tong khar gyis khung yin pe sros rin mang zer ve ku do og nyis sod nam stan zin gyi bu gyud cas par kang sar ka din kyangs pa yin pe gong khod kyi las nor togs rigs dag jan tha dag nas char pa chu dogs kyi phan dogs ced pa las nod tsho sam jor ngan pe thal rigs gel va dang za gyud du nyad pe long ngan sui thad cas pa shar tse ced pa poi lus teng du thims kyi zes non tong nges yin pas de tar mi gos pe chag gyi du don tshad mar zung pe kal pa ze srid par thal rigsu gyu pa pu tsam yang med pa de var nas cug pa gal che che cags to la yar tshes chog du ge par yo dang le la khar tse nas dis...............................

Translation of Tibetan Text

Very brave, protector, cakravarti and Religions king of Ladakh Tsetan Namgyal-order

I order to all the citizens under his kingdom-Ministers, Army officers, other officers especially-kharpon[1], Lonpo[2], Nyerpa[3], Donspon[4], Toga tse[5], chipshon[6] and other people who lookafter Stok village affairs. As a responsible person I pray to God, (Goddess) for the welfare of all human beings. I have constructed Mani wall with two cang cub chortens of its ends[7]. 10 lakh engraved Om Mani Padme Hum mantra slates are placed on (the surface of the Mani wall)[8]. By doing so human beings (can) worship and remember (Tathagat Buddha). Sonam Lhundup Omacik pa of Stok correct all Om Mani Padme Hum (mani) mantras written in Lencha language[9]. I certify his great contribution and (order) to exempt him for 'Bari' an allote him land in Stok village. Give 27 canals land in Thangkok side at the name of Rilmang can. The fuel wood which comes from Rumbak, from it 10 horse load fuel wood to be given to Oma Cikpa house[10].

Notes and References

1. Kharpon : He was the commander of fort (*Tib.Khar*). He excercised many powers and heard cases of judicial nature and dispensed justice. Cf. Datta, C.L.: 'Ladakh and western Himalayan Politics: 1819-1848 (The Dogra conquest of Ladakh, Baltistan and West Tibet and Reactions of other powers); Munshiram Monoharlal Pub.Pvt.Ltd., New Delhi; 1973:36.

2. *Lonpo : Tib.blon-po* or chief municipal and military officer and governor of town. Cf.Datta, C.L., *Op.cit.*: 34.

3. *Nirpa* : *Tib.nyir-pa*: He was the storekeeper in the Ladakh kingdom.

4. *Donspon*: He had higher post of *Goba* and looked the administration of villages of Ladakh.

5. *Toga tse* : He was responsible for storage the grass for Ladakh kingdom animals viz. horses, camels, etc.

6. *Chipspon* : He looked the horses of Ladakh kingdom.

7. *Mani wall with two cang cub* chortens : It is located to the east of new bus stand or towards the east of Radio Station. King Tsetan Namgyal dedicated this Mani wall to his father King Tsewang Namgyal. The structure is 1,957 ft.long, 42 ft. wide and 6 ft. high. The chortens are placed on a 6 ft. high platform towards the ends of the Mani wall. Those chortens are two storey high structures and are square in plan. Both the structure consists of a square tiered base that becomes towards the top and finally culminates into a prayer flag post at the center. There are small niches on the front façade that houses an image of a deity. It consists of random rubble construction and the exteriors are whitewashed. Cf. Sharma, Janhwij : 'Architectural Heritage : Ladakh, The Indian National Trust for Art and Cultural Heritage & Har-Anand Pub. Pvt.Ltd., New delhi; 2003 : 92-93.

8. *Om Mani Padme Hum* : Meaning 'Oh, thou Jewel in the Lotus!, It is the Avalokitesvara mantra. It may more clearly be interpreted lies on the lips of the lotus leaf just as it is going to fall into the lake and be lost in the ocean of water. Cf. Jina, Prem Singh & A.H.Francke:'First Collection of Tibetan Historical Inscriptions on Rock and Stone Ladakh Himalaya'; Satguru Pub. New Delhi; 2003: 147 & Mann, R.S.: 'The Ladakhi : A study of ethnography and change', Anthropological Survey of India, Calcutta, 1986:146.

9. Lencha language: It is more or less equivalent with Sanskrit language.

10. It is said that during King Tsetan Namgyal period villagers carried 50-60 horses load fuel to Stok palace and from this 10 horses load fuel wood was given to Omacik pa house. Cf. Shakarpa, W.D.: 'Political History of Tibet' 'Vol.I, Kalingpong West Bengal Shakappa House, 1976:620.

17

Some Tibetan Inscriptions in Diskit Monastery, Nubra-Leh (Ladakh)

Introduction:

Nubra is a sub-division of Leh district and Diskit is its headquarter. Linguistically Nubra means western portion of Leh i.e. Nubra Nup-west.[1] According to Sanyukta Koshal, the name Nub-ra derived from Idum-ra. Idum means vegetation[2], and 'ra' means a place, or 'place full of vegetation'. Ladakh scholars say it is derived from rdum and ra; rdum means flowers whereas 'ra' to 'valley'; or 'A place (valley) of flowers[3].

Thus, Nubra is a valley with lush green fields, pastures, deserts and thorny bushes surrounded by massive peaks, rocky and snow capped mountains; consisting two main rivers; Nubra and Shayok. The Nubra river joins the shayok near Diskit, after leaving the Chorbat area enters in Baltistan, where it joins with the Indus.

Diskit Monastery

Diskit monastery[4] belongs to Geluk pa tradition of Mahayana Buddhism and was founded in 1420 by lama Cam-sems-Ses-rab-bzang-po, a pupil of Tson-k'a-pa,[5] the founder of Gelukpa order.

The following inscriptions belong to Tson-k'a-pa, and possibly written during the period of his disciple Cam-sems-Ses-rab-bzang-po in 15th century.

Text-1 : Classical language

shar tsong kharu yab da ra kha
che lhu 'abus dang yum
shang mo 'achos kyi sras su ltams
pai tsul lo
ka ma lai dung tu
rab lo gsum pa la rab tu byung
bla ma dan ru ring chen po lam
'agung lo bdun
mai dus su dar
zhus nas mtshan don yod rdo rje
dgas so
bla ma de nyid kzho nu byang thub
chab mdoai mgon pa ru 'aphebs su
dam can srung mai tshogs zhal gzigs pai tshul lo

Text-2: Classical Language

bcom ldan 'adas de bzhin gshegs
pa dgra bcom pa yang dag
par rdzogs pai sangs rgyas dpal rgyal
ba shakya thub pa la
phyag 'atshal lo
skal pa khri phrag gcig gi sdig pa dag go

Text-3 : Classical Language

shes yang rdzun ltar rgan gzhon don
ma rnams 'azhub ji
ltar snyed par bstan pai 'ang 'abyar
mi lus thob 'ajal
'bar stan pai yas ras dang 'ajal dus
'adi bzang gbring bai
kyan ba re gdang song nas no shes
bkrashis dpal

'abyor 'ayal ba mtha ma mkhyen
mkhyen sbyin ba gsal bsong.

Roman Transliteration of the Text-1

shar song kha ru yab da ra kha
che lhu us dang yum
shang mo chos kyi sras su tams
pai tsul lo
ka ma le dung tu
rab lo sum pa la rab tu jung
la ma dan ru rin chen po lam
gung lo dun
me dus su dar
zhus nas chan don yod dorje gas so
la ma de nyid zho nu cang thub
chab doi gon pa ru pheb su
dam can sung me chogs zhal
zigs pe chul lo

Roman Transliteration of the Text-2

com dan das de zhin shegs pa la com
pa yang dag
par zog pe sang gyas pal gyal va
shakya thub pa la
chag shal lo
skal pa thi thag cig gi dig pa dag lo.

Roman Transliteration of the Text-3

shes yang zun tar gan zhon don ma
names zhub ji
tar nyed par stan pe ang jar mi lus
thob jal
bar stan pe yas ras tang jal dus
di zings ding pe
yan ba re dang song nas no shes tasis pal
jor yal va tha ma khyan khyen
cin ba sal song.

Translation of the Text-1

This inscription belongs to shar tsong kha pa[6], father Dar kha che lhu bus[7] and mother shang mo chos[8]. He (perhaps tsong kha pa) became lama near lotus.

The child when attained seven years age, old lama dan ru rin chen[9] gave him (new) name don yod dorje[10] (according to the monastic tradition) guru and zhonu jang thub chab do[11] visited monastery[12]. (then) protectors (of the monastery) appeared in the real form.

Translation of the Text-2

I pray Tathagata Arhat Samyak Sambuddha Sakyamuni. May repent of the sin committed during thousand kalpas.

Translation of the Text-3

To become lama[13] and chomo[14](and) lookafter old men and women,

(by) following vinaya rules (strictly)

(one may) makes (his/her) path of Buddhahood easy.

(There) is no alternative way, therefore, follow (Buddha teachings, monastic rules and vinayic conduct).

Explanation

During 15th century Tsong k'a-pa (or Tsong kha-pa) founded Geluk order, later sent his disciple Cam-sems-ses-rab-bzang-po to Ladakh to spread his doctrine. Accordingly Cam Sems-ses-rab-bzange-po with his assistant came in Ladakh. Dragpa Bum de was then the king of Ladakh, when Cam-sems-ses-rab-bzang-po met him and offered a small statue of Avalokitesvara which was given him by his teacher Tsong-kha-pa, king became happy and asked him to build Buddhist monastery of Gelukpa order anywhere in Ladakh. Subsequently Cam-sems-ses–rab-bzang-po visited Nubra and founded Diskit monastery.

Notes and References

1. Vohra, Rohit: 'Ethno Historical Notes on Nubra in Ladakh'; In : ACTA BIOLOGIA MONTANA,; france, 1985:247.

2. Koshal, Sanyukta: 'Ploughshares of gods : Ladakh; Land, Agriculture and Folk Traditions; Vol.I, Om Pub., New Delhi; 2001:13.

3. Vohra, Rohit: 'Ethno Historical Notes on Nubra in Ladakh'; op.cit.: 247.

4. Diskit monastery: It is situated on a rock near Diskit.

5. Tson-k'a-pa (Tsong-kha-pa) : In 1368, the last Mongol emperor was expelled by the founder of the Ming dynasty. Thereafter, the emperors of this dynasty tried to bring Tibet under Chinese Govt. control so that they could send gifts to Sakya lama time and again. However, Sakya lama understand the Chinese policy, consequently to prevent the predominance of any monastery, a decision was taken under which head of monasteries made equal rank to the Sakya lama. This facilitated the great reform which Lamaism underwent in the time of the Emperor Jong lo, a reform brought about by the celebrated Tsong-kha-pa. Infact Tsong-kha-pa was born in 1357 in Amdo. At the process of time, he set out to Tibet to acquire knowledge of Buddhism from the original sources. He started *parmita* texts from kungpad, *Abhidharma* from Je Rendawa, *vinaya*' from Khachen losal, Madhyamica from Narthans & Kaminpa and *Mahamudra* from Gampopa. Later felt the need to purify and reform the discipline of Mahayana Buddhism. In 1409 he built Galdan monastery on a hill near Lhasa. He was the first Abbot of this monastery and preached his followers to strictly follow the monastic discipline. In 1419, he got *parinirvana*. His tradition later known by 'Yellow School' or 'Gelukpa' order. Cf.William, M. Monier: 'Buddhism', Chowkhamba, Varanasi; 1964: 277.

6. shar tsong kha pa= Je Tsong kha pa

7. Dar kah che lhu bus = Lubum-ge. He was the father of Je Tsong kha pa.

8. shang mo chos=She was the mother of Je Tsong kha pa.

9. Lama dan ru rin chen =Or Chorje Tondum Rinchen : He was the teacher of Je Tsong kha pa.

10. don yod dorje : This name was given him by his guru for receiving the basic Buddhist education and training under his guidance.

11. zhonu jang thub chab do : He was the main disciple of Tsong-kha-pa.

12. Monastery : It would be Gaidan monastery

13. Lama : Buddhist monk.

14. Chomo : Buddhist nun.

18

Phokarzong (Tib.Pho-kar-dzong) : A Meditation Cave

On 15th September 2000 morning I alongwith my some students started journey for Phokarzong[1]. It is situated in Purig of Ladakh region. We reached there late evening about 9:30 o'clock and, took halt at the community hall at Shargol[2] which is 220 km from Leh. In Ladakh, I found community hall almost in every village, therefore, it helped me whenever I visited remote villages for research work. Here follows the details of villages through which I passed before reaching Phokarzong.

Leh[3]
|
Nemo[4]
|
Basgo[5]
|
Saspol
|
Lardo[6]
|
Ula tokpo[7]

|
Hemis chu[8]
|
Nurla[9]
|
Khaltse (or Khalsi)[10]
|
Langru[11]
|
Lamayuru[12]
|
Larsa[13]
|
Photola[14]
|
Chepkhang chan Hanasku[15]
|
Bodhkharbu[16]
|
Khangra[17]
|
Namkila[18]
|
Vado[19]
|
Wakha[20]
|
Mulbek[21]
|
Shargol
|
Phokarzong

Next day from Shargol we climbed for Phokarzong through the narrow nala, about two and half hour climbing, arrived Phokarzong. It is a peaceful place, situated in a narrow valley between high mountains of Wakha, Mulbek and Phokar at about

13,000 ft. from the sea level. In olden days many high ranked Buddhist saints, yogis including Padmasambhava[22] used to come for meditation.

The Phokarzang is a largest complex of several caves connected by small passages contains two chortens, a small stone image of a peaching Buddha and a four armed Avalokitesvara[23] made of marble Besides there are several carvings, foot-prints etc. The foot print of Padmasambhava impressed on the ceiling of the cave is an important example. Buddhist Mantras e.g. 'Om, Ah Hung', Om Mani Padma Hum', Om Ah Hum', Vajra Guru Padma Siddhi Hum' etc. are some engraved important mantras which can be seen here and there in the caves (Appendix 18.1). To sum up I would say Phokarzong as a meditation center of Yogis, famous throughout in Ladakh, annually thousands Buddhist pilgrims visit the site. Here follows the details:

Ma-Ra-Ta-ke: it is found in the main trunk of Phokarzong cave. At Ma-Ra-Ta-ke Guru Rinpoche used to sit for meditation. Nearby holy filtered water comes out from the rock on every auspicious days i.e. 8, 10, 25 and 30th of the month of Tibetan calendar (Appendix).

Rin sum gonpo: On the way inside the cave we can see Rig sum gonpo[24] syambhu engraved figures (Appendix 18.1).

Syambhu Hole : There is a symbhu[25] hole in the cave, which is known 'Tang-Mo-Lok-Par'. On its top 'yung-dung'[26] are engraved. However, only lucky person can see them. The number of 'yung-dung' vary in between three to seven, depending on the luck of person.

Changcub-chorten: The Changcub chorten[27] of this cave has spiritual significance as whosoever pass through this may get rid from the wheel of life or Bhava cakra.

Snake Carvings: When Padmasambhava was meditating here, some Nagas attacked Nagaraj. However, Padmasambhava with his spiritual power saved his life and killed his enemies who came in Nagas form. The snake carvings are the symbol of Nagas and are beautifully carved in the cave (Appendix 18.1).

Khando-ma hair : We can often see some strange hair of goddess Khando-ma . They are found in black and white forms (Appendix 18.1).

Tung-Fakh and sol-Thap: In the cave we may come across syambhu Tung-fakh and Sol-Thap. Nonetheless on the top of these there is a ruined fort (Appendix 18.1).

Sing-dong-ma: Besides other religious important things we can see sing-dong-ma, riding on a white horse (Appendix 18.1).

Historical Background : Drup-Thop Urgyan visited Phokarzong during 13th century A.D., later retreat in the cave for three months. One night in dream he saw something burning other site of the cave. He went there, but didn't find anything. Next day he once again went there. This time he had doubt and dug the spot. Soonafter he found a strange marble statue of Avalokitesvara. It is about 6 inches in height and is displayed annually during Phokarzong Tse-chu festival.

Zimsung of Phokarzong

The Zimsung was earlier at the top of the mountain, and it is swept to the near the Phokarzong cave (Fig 18.1).

Phokarzong Tukpe (Tib.Dubpe) Gonpa

The Phokarzong Tukpe temple is popularly known Chenrezik Lhakhang (Fig. 18.2).

1. Khanpo

2. Padmasambhava

3. Yabsras sum[28]

4. Chenresik[29]

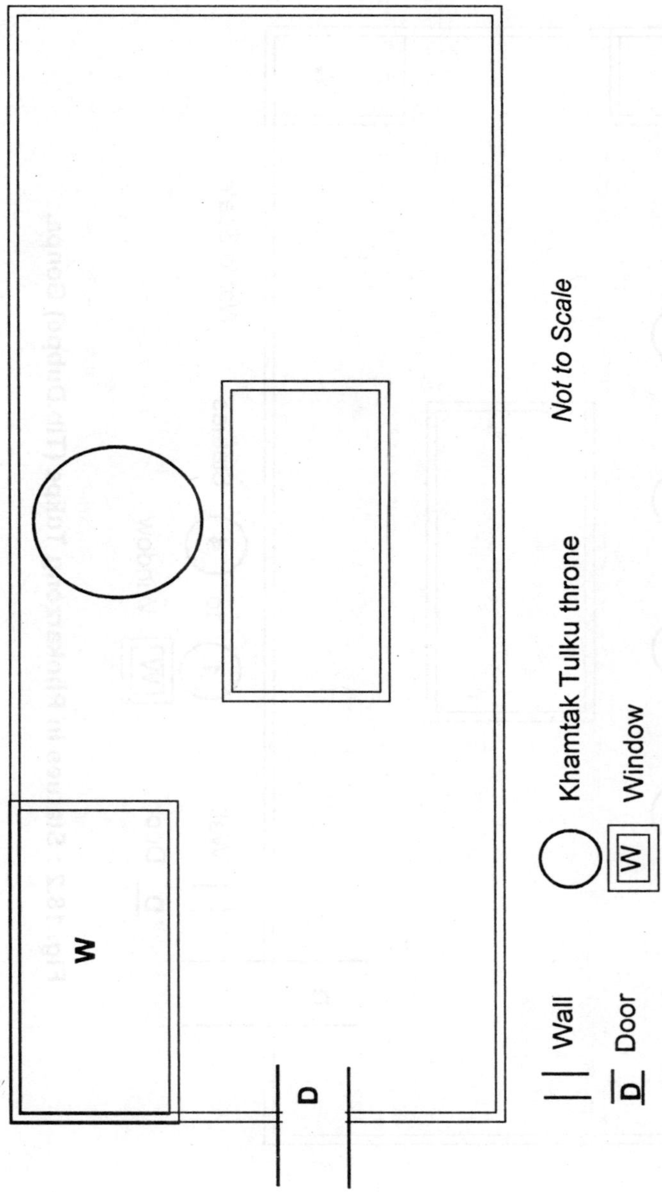

Fig.18.1 : Zimsung in Phokarzong.

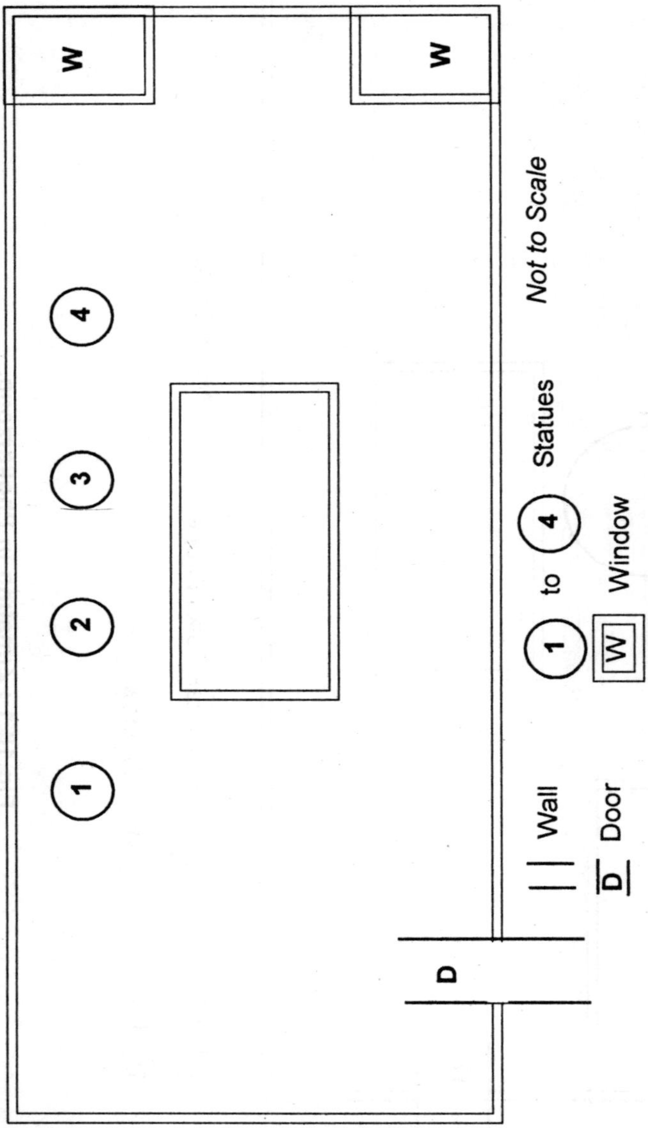

Fig. 18.2 : Statues in Phokarzong Tukpe (Tib.Dubpe) Gonpa.

Padmasambhava Gonpa

Padmasambhava temple has principle statue of Padmasambhava (Fig. 18.3).

(C) ; Centre statue – Padmasambhava

1. Padmasambhava (or Padma Samnla) or Guru Tho-ao
   - Seated
   - Height : one foot

2. Stag tsang Ras pa[30] : A great siddha of Drugpa
   - Height : One foot

3. Lama Dorje chang[31] :
   - seated
   - height : one foot and six inches

4. Buddha :
   - Holds dorje
   - Standing Posture

Right side up of the center statue

5. Buddha : height –1'
6. Unknown : Height –1/2'
7. Padmasambhava : Height – 1-1/2'
8. Unknown : Height –1/2'

Right side down of the center statue

9. Avalokitesvara : Height-1-1/2'
10. Unknown : Height- ½'
11. Dorje[32] : Height 1.5'
12. Unknown : ?

Left side down of the center statue

13. Unknown : ?
14. Chorten[33]
15. Unidentified.

Administrative Control

Phokarzong Tukpe and Padmasambhava temple are under the Hemis monastery and belong to Drugpa k'agyud order. Both these don't have frescos like other Buddhist gonpas in Ladakh.

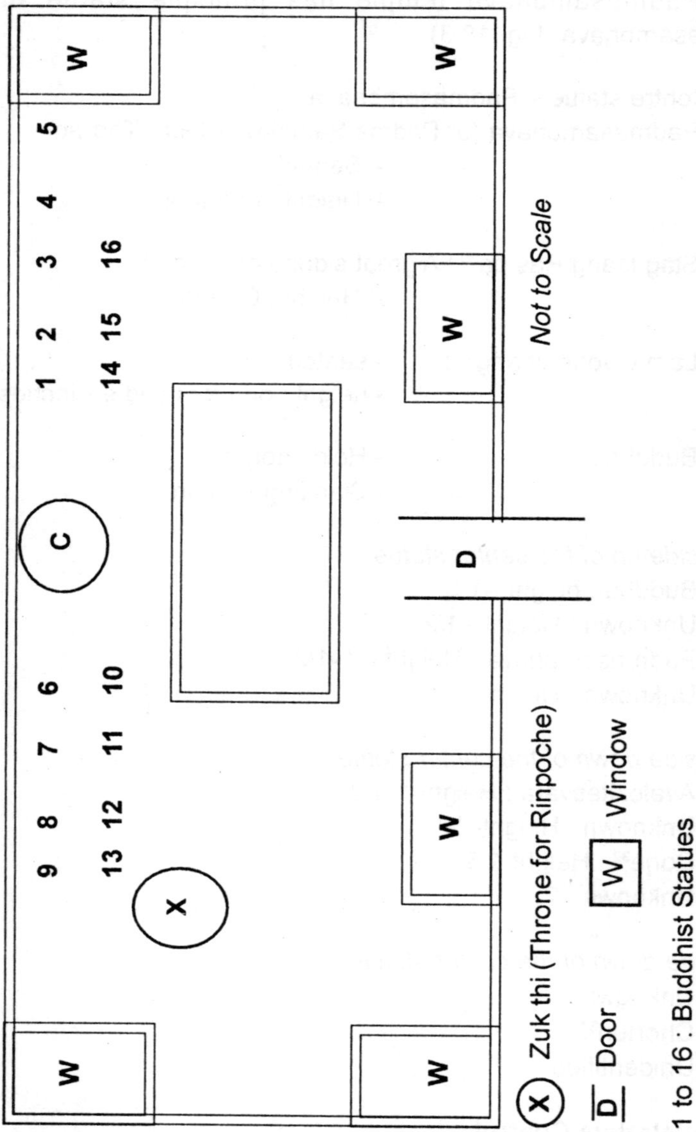

Fig. 18.3. Statues in the Padmasambhava Gonpa of Phokarzong.

Notes and References

1. Phokarzong : It is village near Shargol above to this famous Phokarzong cave is situated where many yogis in olden days came for meditation.

2. Shargol : Lat 34°24'
Long 76°22'
Elev. 10, 29'
A village about 100 houses on the left bank of Wakha river.

3. Lat : Lat 34°10'
Long 77°37'
Elev. 11,500'

   It is the Leh district headquarter of Ladakh; is situated about 8 kms. from the right bank of the Indus River. Cf. Gazetteer of Kashmir and Ladakh, Vivek Pub., Delhi,1974: 562.

4. Nemo (or Nimo) : Lat 34°12'
Long 77°20'

   A village on the right bank of the Indus River, about 70 kms below Leh, and opposite the junction of the Zanskar River. It is on the road of Kargil to Leh. Summers are pleasant in Nemo. Cf. Gazetteer of Kashmir and Ladakh, op.cit.: 763.

5. Basgo : Lat 30°14'
Long 77°20'

   It is situated on the right bank of Indus River, about 50 kms below Leh. It is one Buddhist monastery in which chamba or Future Buddha statue is famous throughout in Ladakh, it is one of the biggest statue in Ladakh.

6. Lardo : It is near Saspol village, has 30-50 houses.

7. Ula takpo : Next to Lardo also has a few houses.

8. Hemis chu : It is quite a good number of houses.

9. Nurla : It is just before Khaltse and has a good camping side.

10. Khaltse (or Khalsi) : Lat 34°19'
Long 75°57'
Elev. 10, 130'

It is a big village has about 150-200 houses, situated on the right bank of the Indus, about 170 kms below Leh. It is a halting place on the Leh-Kargil road. During Dogra war Dogras built 77 feet long and 8 feet broad bridge on Indus River, near one small fort was also built. Cf. Gazetteer, op.cit. 360-61.

11. Langru : This village comes next to Khalatse, and has small population.

12. Lamayuru: It is a big village on way to Leh to Kargil. In olden kardari or collectorate collected revenue for the following villages- Lamaguru, Wanla, Photaksa, Velchung and Lingshet; Lamayuru was the biggest village and about Rs. 2,200/- cash revenue was collected from the above village per year, besides taxes in kind not being recorded. Cf. Gazetteer of Kashmir and Ladakh; op.cit: 555.

13. Larsa : It is a small village near Lamayaru.

14. Photola : (Also called Fotu La)

It is a mountain pass on the road between Lamayuru and Kargil.

15. Chapkhang chan Hanasku: It is a village on the road between Khalatse and Bodhkharbu.

16. Bodhkharbu : Lat 34°20'
Long. 76°37'
Elev. 11,890'

This village is situated between the Namkila and Photola (or Fotula). Cf. Gazetteer; op.cit.: 360.

17. Khangra : It is a small village before Namkila pass (13,000' elevation).

18. Namkila : Lat 34°22'
Long 76°35'
Elev. 13,000'

It crossed between Shergol and Kharbu on the Leh to Kargil road. The ascent from the west is very gradual, and is 5 miles long. A spring of fresh water about half way up. An easy descent down to Kharbu. Cf. Gazetteer; op.cit.: 619.

19. Vado : It is a small village near Namkila (pass).

20. Wakha : Lat 34°25'
Long 76°25'
Elev. 11,000'

A village on the right bank of the Wakha river, situated west of the Namkila. In 1820-22 when Moorcraft visited Ladakh said:

" Barley is cultivated here, there are about 50 houses". Cf. Gazetteer op.cit.: 848.

21. Mulbek : Lat 34°23'
Long 76°25'

Here a monastery and village is situated on the right bank of the Paskhyum river (or Wakha chu) and passed between Shergol and Kharbu-on the Leh-Kargil road. It is four miles from. Cf. Gazetteer; op.cit.: 610.

22. Padmasambhava : He was the great mystic saint from India who had tremendous miraculous powers. He brought Buddhist Tantra in Tibet in the 8th century A.D. and introduced its learning and practice.He rubued the local deities and demons who were obstructing the construction of Samyas monastery. Cf. Lobzang Tsewang : Sakyamuni', CIBS; 2001 : 26.

23. Avalokitesvara: He is the Buddha of Compassion, he is the manifestation of the Buddha on the enjoyment body, is the chief Bodhisattva of Mahayana Buddhism. He is seated in cross-legged posture. He is the Buddhisattva of kindness and compassion. Cf.S.K. Das: Tara. C.I.B.S. 2003: 26.

24. Rig sum gonpo : It is a group of three deities e.g.
    (1) Avalokitesvara (White colour)
    (2) Vajrapani (Blue colour)
    (3) Manjusri (Red colour)

25. Syambhu : Which is formed by nature not by man.

26. Yung-dung: Swastika, a auspicious symbol.

27. Changcub chorten : Correctly spell as byavi-c'ub mc'od rten and means "chorten of illumination." It has a square base with one or more steps round the foot, above this is a round drum, the bum pa or pot, above again are thirteen umbrellas.

28. Yabsras sum : The group of three great lamas viz.
    (1) Tsong-khapa (Guru or teacher)
    (2) Gyal tsab (disciple)
    (3) Khasdup (disciple)

29. Chenresik : The lord who looks down with compassion, is a manifestation of Amitabha, is shown in white colour, has 'Om Mani Padme Hum' as his mantra.

30. Stag tsang Ras pa : (1574-1651), the famous Drug-pa siddha who, worked in western Tibet in the time of the Ladakhi kings Jamyang Namgyal (1595-1616), Sengge Namgyal (1616-1642) and Deldan Namgyal (1647-1694) Cf. Finegan Jack; 'Tibet : A Dreamt of Image,; Tibet House, 1986: 204.

31. Lama Dorje chang : Tib. Rdo-rje 'chang sometimes begins with the Heruka.

32. Dorje : Probably it would be Chhana Dorje, called Vajrapani, holder of the thunderbolt.

33. Chorten : In Hindi called stupa; literally means an "offering holder"

APPENDIX 18.1

PHOKARZONG MANUSCRIPT (TIBETAN) TEXT IN CLASSICAL LANGUAGE

Phu mkhar rjong gi gnas bshad dga snang chu zl 'ai 'aod dgar zhes bya ba bzhugs so ao a'a: h' aum bdzra gru ru nghe mra-kke ni ye : na mo n'a ma/

'ae m'a ho/

'azhi thog dang po'ai chos sku kun tu bzang/

'od min spros bral blo'adas brjod tu med/

'akhar 'adas gnyis med spang blang re dog/

snang stong dbyer med kun bzang yab yum bstod/

a'a ÷ las pad dkar zla gdan h'au yig las/

bla mdo rje sems dp'a gngas ri sku/

de la nyi shar phog lhar 'aod zer gyi/

sdig sbyang longs sku rdo rje sems dp'a bstod/

mngal gyi ma gos pdm'ai dkyil nas 'akhrungas/

rkhya bod lha srin bhul b'ai mthu stobs can/

bod dang la dvags 'agro ba thams cang gyi gtsug nor pad 'abyung sprul p'ai sku la bstod/

sngon tshe rig 'adzin nus ltan rdo rje 'achang/

ma 'aong dbe gshegs mos pa mth'a yas zhabs/

da lta pad 'abyung rgyal tshabs 'abrog ban ngos/

'ajigs bral ye shes rdo rje sbyi bor mchod/

phyogs bsu bcu dus gsum rgyalba sras bcas kyi/

thugs rje ye shes gcig tu bsdus b'ai mgon blag gi drin can rtse b'ai bla ma rnams/

mi bral spyi bo'ai gtsug gi rgyan tu bzhug/ de yan chag kyi mchod brjod kyi me tog song nas/da gnas bshad byed pa po 'ai rgyu mtsar dkod pa ni/

Aom a'a ÷ h'aum ÷ h'aum nag 'abr dang myang pan gting 'abzin bzang/

sprul p'ai sku mchog 'aj'a mtson snying po yis/

skye a phreng yin rlom pad 'aphreng ltar brgynd pa/

gnas yig bkod p'ai chos rje rtogs ldan ngas/

ma 'aong blo dman rang dang skal mnyam la/

phan p'ai blo yi la dvags gsham phyogs nang phu mkhang ao rgan rdzong gi grub gnas kyi/

sngon gyi gnas yig yod zhes rgan rab kyis/

bshang kyang la dvags phyi nang sa mtsams lang/

sngon dus la dvags chos rgyal gong ma rnams/

'ab' al ti dpon dang phan tsun nang 'akhrugs yongs/

byed nas gnas dang gtsug lag khang la sogas/

mthor rkyen 'abyung ba snga rab rnams kyis bshad/

de phyir gnas bshad gang yang mi 'adug go/

dad ldan 'agro rnams gnas mjal mchod 'abul la/

phebs mi rnams la gnas 'adi lo rgyus dang/rang 'abyon rnams kyang mkhyed par 'adod na yang/

gnas bshad med p'ai dad mos byed nas log/

chu mdun sleb kyang skom sel ma 'abyed par/

stong log 'agro ba ji bzhin snying rje/

bsam nas ma 'aong gnas mjal rnams kyi don/

gnas bshad rin chen 'aphreng ba bdag gis spel/

gnas bshad dag snang 'adi ltaro/

'abyung ba gsum ladan chu mo bya lo/

bod rab 'abyung bu bdun pa/

rab lo 966 sbyi lo 1993 bod da bzhi b'ai tshes nyi shu spyi zla drug p'ai ches nyin phu mkhar yul gyi yul spyi nas ayon rjong gi sgrub sde gso mi'a rab gnas la ngas shad zhu b'ai dus gnas nang ayon tshogs khang chen po'ai nang tsig bdun gsol 'adebs (grangs) sogs dang bdzra gu ru khri tshar 30,000 bcas gu ru rin po che la gsol ba 'adebs bzhin nyi m'ai chu tshod gnyis nas mtsan gyi chu tshod bcu dang phyed par tu phyag bchod dang 'abred b'ai rang nyid gcig bu mthun la sdad pa yin/

bod tses nyi shu gcig nyin 'abri 'abrug bla ma dge 'adun bcu phrag dang btshun ma bcas sgrub sde tshogs khang nang tshogs 'akhor brgya mchod sogs phul nas bkra shis rab gnas dang 'aprin 'acol sogs phul yin/

ngos rang grub phug lte bar mthun la sdod skabs rang gi bsam pa la sngon lo stong phag sngon la sngas rgyas gnyis pa ayon rin po che 'adir phebs nas byis rlabs mdzad pa bskal pa bzang kyang da lta gnas 'adi la gnas bshad gsal po zhig 'abyung na dad ldan rnams la phan pa dang sngas rgas kyi bstan pa yang/

dar bar nges basm zhing ayon rin po che la gsol ba 'adebs bzhin gnas/

bar skabs zhig la nyid la song ba lta bu zhig 'abyung rang la rmi lam zhig mthong ngos rang sngags 'achang rdo rje 'adzin p'ai che lugs byed nas phyag gyas la ta ma ru dar sna lnga (ldan) phyag gyon na snang srid gsal b'ai me long zhig rin po che du m'ai rgyan dang ldan pa dar dkar ring ba dang bcas pa thog nas/

lho nub phyogs kyi thang chen (gser) po zhig la 'agro skabs/

thang dkyil du chu mig dvangs gsal yid du 'aong ba zhig gi sar s'leb/

der nga rang ngal nas kha skom nas chu zhig btung ngo bsam nas 'athung bzhin p'ai skabs mdun du mkh'a 'agro ma dar dkar lha lhub gyon pa zhig phyag gyas na nor gzong dang gyon nas shel dkar gyi 'aphing ba bsnams pa zhig 'abyung/

bu nga ngo shes sam zhes gsungs/

rang nyid nas sems ha cang dg'a ba zhig la gnas skabs gang yang zhu ma thub/

de ma thag ngos kyi sems la nga skya ba sngon dus kong po'ac yul du gter ston 'aj'a tshon snying po'ai skye ba 'agyur skabs kyi ma de 'ai rdo rje gyu sgron m'ai sprul pa yin pa de rang yi ma yin par ngo shes/ ngos kyi aa ma la red zhus yin/

'ao de rang yin/da mi lo mang po 'adas p'ai rjes su la dvags phyi nang sa mtshams su ayon gyi gnas p'au rig phug (mo)/

che gnas 'adir bu rang dang phrad pa nga re skyid/gsungs/

nor gzhong de nga la gnang/

da khyed rang gi 'adod pa ltar gnas 'adi bshad pa ngas byed chog/

dran pa ma brjed pa (yin) la gzung shig/gsungs nas dghyes 'adzum mdangs dang bcas nga la gzig/

ngos rang yang ma bu phrad pa ltar dg'a ba 'abyung nas (ta) ma ru rgyan ldan ma la phul nyin/

ma nas bu rang gi me long legs pa de nang ltos gsungs nas/

ng'ai me long nang ltas nas sdad skabs/

ayon rdzong gi gnas ri thams cad phra lham gyi shar/

lo rgyus kyi rda yig yang gsal/

'ao da bu rang gi me long nang ji lta ba bzhin gzugs brnyan brag ris dang grub phug gi chags tshul (bdybabs) sogs leng par bris/

ma 'aong dad ldan rnams la bshod/

da nga rang lho nub bzang mtog dpal ri ayon rin po che drung du 'agro 'ao gsung nas ngos kyi mgo la phyag gyas p'ai bshad nas rjes su ma bu gnyis mjal 'aong gsung mi snang bar 'agyur ro/da me long nang gi gnas bshad bkod pa ni.

ae ma ho ÷

ao rgyan ma ra (tkki) brag rdzong 'adi ÷

(sngon) dus sngs rgyas gnyis pa pdma 'abyung ÷

ao rgyan yul dang aa sh'a 'abru gling yul ÷

zangs gling kha che yul sogs byin rlabs skabs : lo ni gcig stong dgu brgya gcig dus : kha che yul gyi rgyal po gho b'ai na : lus la klu yi nad kyi gzung b'ai dus : sngags dang sman sogs (gang) yang ma phan nas : ao rgyan yul nas pdma 'abyung gnas zhus : de tus rta mgrin yang gsang dkyil 'akhor bsham : rgyal por dbang gad sa bdag gdon las grol : pad 'adyung rje la rgyal rab dad nas ÷ 'a sh'a 'abru sha yul dang ghil dhi'ai yul ÷ mchod p'ai nas su phul nas pad 'abyung dang ÷ rgyal po gho b'ai n'a bcas gnas 'adir phebs ÷ ao rgyan rdzong la p'au rig phug mo zar ÷ klu bdud h'a la nag po gnas sa yin ÷ kha che rgyal la klu 'adi gnod pa na ÷ ao rgyan' adir phebs dan la btags pa yin ÷ rta phyag khyung gling zhes p'ai brag ri 'adi ÷ grub phug chen po 'ai gyon la yod pa yin ÷ brag gi leb la gshing rje chos rgyal gyi ÷ me long 'aj 'a ldan 'abur la mjal ba yod ÷ de'ai steng khro bo rta mgrin gsal ba yod ÷ rta mgrin gyas la rgya gar (pan) chen ni ÷ p'ai ma mitra 'ai sku gzugs gyoni gzigs yod ÷ de'ai aog na mkh'a 'agro seng gdong yod ÷ de'ai' aog la rjo gyu sgron la ÷ gtsho mo che la phyag na md'a dar bsnam ÷ gyon la mkh'agro chung ba gnyis gzhugs yod ÷ brag ri gzhung la bk'a brgyad bde adus sku ÷ gsal bar bzhags yod de'ai mdun ngos naje btsun mi la sgom thag rang sgrig bzhugs ÷ de'ai sten na rgyal ba rgyod tshangs bzhugs ÷ de nas gyas kyi brag nag dmar po'ai bar ÷ 'abri gung skyob ba 'ajig rten mgon po (bzhug) ÷ de'ai steng na rdo rje 'achang chen yot ÷ bk'a brgyad gyod gyimth'a m'ai brag leb na ÷ bk'a brgyad yongs kyi bstan srung lha mo yot ÷ de 'ai rtse la shug p'ai dbu gdugs yod ÷ de'ai steng na brag zur ngo 'ajam la ÷ padma dkar po'ai sku brnyan gsal ba yod ÷ ri rta bar sangs rgyas bstan pa yis ÷ spyin bdag ha shang ha phrug skor ba yod ÷ gshin rje chos rgyal me long gyon phyogs na ÷ dus gsum sangs rgyas sku bryan gsal bar yod ÷ de ai 'aog (ma) gnas srung ma mo dam can dang ÷ gz'a chen khyab 'ajug dbu dgu ldan pa yod ÷ de nas lung p'ai pho brang dbu rtse la ÷ 'adzag p'ai lam na klu bdud cho 'aphrul gyi ÷ sbral gyi gzugs brnyan rin thung bdun brgyud yod de na yar la song nas rta mgrin phug ÷ phyag rdor phug zhes phug pa gnyis 'abrel yod ÷ de'ai nang gdon zhi b'ai bzang drug sman ÷ mdog bzhin sa sngays byin rlabs ldan pa yod ÷ sa sngayas nang nas ao rgyan rin po che ÷ dbu skra dkar po mkh'agro ma tsho rgyal gyi ÷ dbu skra nag po byin rlabs skabs rin thob ÷ phub gnyis gyas na bya khyung ga ru tra ÷ sku yi gzugs brnyan brag la thim pa yod ÷ de rnams klu bdud btul b'ai rtags ni yin ÷ kha che yul gyi rgyal po gho b'ai n'ai ÷ nad las sgrol b'ai lo rgyus bzhin du ni ÷ rang byon rnams rta phyag gling la gzigs ÷ rtogs ldan mchog sprul sngags 'aching dkon mchog thub bstan p'ai rgyal mtsan gyi gnas bshad gsar du phye b'ai le'au dang po'ao ÷ rta phyag gling gi dbu rtse ri de ni ÷ yi dam gsang ba 'adus p'ai pho brang yin ÷ de'ai mdun na shar gyi skar khung zhes ÷ brag la 'au khang yod pa ngo tshar bzhuga ÷ pho brang lte ba rdo rje ke'au tshang 'adi ÷ chags tshul rim ba cung zhig 'adar bshad na ÷ pho brang mtshan la ma r'a (tkki'ai) rdzong ÷ dbyibs ni phyi ltar (tsitta'ai) dbyibs su yong ÷ tsitta'ai dbyibs 'aog pho brang zla gam gjugs ÷ dbang gi dkyil 'akhor thab dang 'adra ba yod ÷ de'ai jur tsam pho brang lte ba yi ÷ brag phug sten 'aog gnyis ldan byin rlabs can ÷ ao rgyan jla bdan zhag dbun gting 'adzin bzhugs ÷ mkha 'agra'ai am yig me long nang na gsal ÷ brag phug nang ni mi yi byang 'akhog bzhin ÷ spyi bo bde chen 'akhor lo'ai rtsa'adbas yod ÷ mgrin pa lonsbyod 'akhor lo'ai tsa 'adabs yod ÷ snying kha chos kyi 'akhor lo 'ai tsa 'adabs yod ÷ snying gi thad du gu ru'ai tshe bum gyi ÷ rang byon shin tu gsal ba mjal rgyu yod ÷ ao rgyan rin po che yi tsha sgrub ni ÷ yang gsang nyi zla g'au' ai tshe sgrub mdzad ÷ pad rgyal phyi nang ksang p'ai sgrub khog dang ÷ byang sems dkar dmar gter rjas khyad 'aphags sogs ÷ .... gter rnams yod pa me long nang nas gsal ÷gter bdag klu bdud rdo rje gyu sgron dang ÷ bk'a srun gsum gyi bya ra byed bzhin yod ÷ phur brgyud b'au ti yang gsang 'adus pa dang ÷ sgru phur phur rdzas rig phung kun grol gyi ÷ dam rdzas khyad 'aphgs gnas nang bzhugs pa yod ÷ ma'aong gter ston————zhes bya 'abyang 'agyur na ÷ rten 'adel 'adzom zhing par chad med na phebs ÷ ai de 'aog lte ba sprul p'ai 'akhor lo yod ÷ brla gyas brla gyon rub dbyibs bu kha gnyis ÷ phan tshun 'agro b'ai brag phug 'adi gnyis yin ÷ gsang gnas bde skyong 'akhor lo'ai dbyibs sgo nas ÷ phyi la thon p'ai brag phug rgya sgo yin ÷ rgyab kyi rtsa khung phug b'ai gyas ltag nas ÷ rtog ldan ngos kyi phyag rjes gsom yod ÷ 'agro rnams dpal rir ao rgyan chen po'ai drung ÷ mjal b'ai rten 'abrel sgrig p'ai smon lam yin ÷ gsang snags dma rdzas mang du 'abyung ba de ÷ 'agro ba su yi spyod kyang ngan song med ÷ sgrub chu 'chu 'achi med bdud rtsi rgyun bbas 'adi ÷ tshes bcu dus mchod rnams la mang bar 'abyung ÷ bdu rtses shug pa gdugs kyi bdyibs can yod ÷ de 'ai stong na bstan srung byag men yod ÷ pho brang lte ba brag phug ma r'a (tkk'ai) rdzong gi gnas bashad le' au gnyis p'ao ÷ pho brang gnas kyi lte b'ai gyas phyogs na ÷ rta mgrin phyag rdor gling gi 'aog gi brag ÷ dbus na mtsho rgyal phug pa zhes bya yod ÷ de'ai nang ao rgyan pdm'ai sku rjes yod ÷ de nas gyon la'ajam dbyangs ral gri yod ÷ sku rjes mdun na mkh'agro'ai tshogs 'akor yod ÷ tshogs chang bdut rtsi bar med bbas pa yod ÷ de nas yar 'agro mar babs lam kha na ÷ byang chub mchod rten rang byon gsal ba yod ÷ mchod rten te steng 'agro ba su 'agro na ÷ tshe 'adi sdig spyang shi na ngan song med ÷ rig drug gnas 'adren byen dang 'adra b'ao ÷ de'ai gyas na las 'abras dkar nag gi ÷ dge steg dkar nag rtags p'ai grag khung gnyis ÷ gcig nas 'adzul nas gcig nas thon sa yod ÷ mi (grot med par thar na las dag yin ÷ par la rtsir b'ai pi pi rdo rje yod ÷ de yio rtsir na sdig pa bshags la 'abad ÷ de la ma thog las ni yang ba yin ÷ deng sang mi rnams gyi drag po log pa zer/

dg'a ba sgom nas dge la btson par bya ÷ byang chub sems dang ma'abral brtan por bzdung de'ai 'aog na gting 'adzin phug pa yod ÷ ajam dbyangs sgrub na shis (rab) rbyur du 'aphel ÷ de'ai sten ÷ yar la mthon po brag kyib na ÷ yar ngo mar ngo'ai tshes grangs rtags p'ai phyuir ÷ 卐 gyung drung tshal la bris ldan pa shar bzhin yod ÷ yar ngo tshas gcig nas ni bco lng'ai bar ÷ 卐 gyung drung dbun shar shin tu gsal ba yod ÷ marngo bau drug nas ni nam gang bar ÷ rim gyi rim gyi med par 'agyur ba yin ÷ yees mcho rgyal brag phug 'aog 'aog nas ÷ brag nag lab la gzhi bdag jo mo ni ÷ spun gsun gzugs kyi ri mo rang byon yod ÷ de nas yi ge aom a'a ha'aum gsum yod ÷ slar yang aom a'a h'aum gsum ni ÷ tseg nas yod p'ai rang byon ngo mtshar yod ÷ gu rus byin rlabs mdzad pa 'abru gsum yin ÷ kha che chos rgyal gho b'ai n'a la ni ÷ dbang gzhi bsgyur cir sku gsum ngo sprod nas ÷ ao rgyan bla slob lta ba dbyen med 'agyur ÷ dgongs gla bde byer med 'agyur ÷ dgongs klong dbyed med 'agyur b 'ai 'agru gsum yin ÷ kha che chos rgyal gho b'ai n'a yi dus ÷ yi ge rang byon rda yig gsal po yod ————yi ge gzugs ni del ltar mjal rgyu yod ÷ rgyal po'adi yi mng'a 'aog rgyal bstan dar ÷ gnas 'ade 'ai yan lag kh'a (pal) kar jo'ang yod ÷ de'ai gyas na bdzra gu ru dang ÷ yig drug vang byon shin tu gsal pa yod ÷ de 'aog shug stong chen po'ai nye 'adbas na ÷ gu ru phyag rjes zhabs rjes gsal bar yon ÷ gnas la 'agro b'ai lam gyi gyas phyogs na ÷ brag mdog dang ser ngo 'ajam leb la ni bk'a gdam mchod rten bang rim can zhig yod ÷ cung zhig 'aong nas shug sdong chen po yig ÷ de ni chos rgyal sku lng'ai lha shug yin ÷ de'ai mdun na thu mig yan lag brgyad ÷ 'athung bas stig byang lh'ai bdud rtsi yod ÷ de nas yar la lung p'ai nang song nas mgon khang phug zer bya rog rang yod ÷ bstan bsrung ma h'a k'a li'ai skrub gnas yin ÷ de'ai sting gi ri bo tshogs zhing dbyibs bk'a brgyud bla ma rdo rje 'a chang chen nas ÷ te lo (n'a) ro mar mi dvags po sogs ÷ bzhugs p'ai bk'a brgyud pho brang zhes su grags ÷ de'ai gyas na brag ni dgon p'ai dbyibs ÷ gling gi ga sar rgyal po 'ai pho brang yin ÷ mdun na mi chen langas 'adr'ai brag gcig yod ÷ de ni gling gi dp'a bo mdan ma yin ÷ deng sang hal gyi la ni zer ba mul bhi rong la'agro sa na yod/

da gyas gnas bstan bcu drug brag ri yod ÷ de nas bde mchog 'akar lo 'apho brang yod ÷ de'ai gyas na byang sems chen po/

brgyẹd ÷ bzhugs p'ai brag ri ngo mtshar che ba yod ÷ de'aog brag ri kun dg'a ra b'ai nang ÷ spyan ras gzigs sku phyag stong spyan stong yod ÷ de'ai nas zur brag dkar ngo 'ajam la ÷ bstam srung a'a phyi melong bsnam pa yod ÷ de nas brag ri tshogs kyi dbyibs lta bur ÷ ngo la mchod me rang byon khyad par yod ÷ sgrub sde dgon nas tshan la mjal na kun gyi gsal po mjal zhing bde mo mthong ÷ (sa ri rtse phu) lung chen pu ni spyan ras gzigs dbang gi ÷ pho brang po ta la zhes tshan tu gsol ÷ sngon dus rgyal ba rgodo tshangs slob ma mchog ÷ ayom kha che yul nas 'ader 'aphebs nas ÷ sa ri lung nang mthams khang byin ldan nang ÷ zla ba bsum dang phyed kha lhag tsam bzhugs ÷ grub chen ao rgyan gter nas (gzhes) p'ai sku ÷ rang byon k'a ma ru p'ai spyan ras gzigs ÷ phyag bzhi pa de 'ai byin rlabs shin tu che ÷ 'agro ba su yi mjal yang ngan song med ÷ sa chu rdo la me 'abar sogs kyang yod ÷ sa ri nang gi mtshams khang dang grub thob ayon phebs 'adug zla ba bsum lhag bzhags p'ai(lo)(rgus) de me long nang gi dag snang bris pa yin/

lung chen nang gi mchod rten bang rim can ÷ ri de rgya gar mchod rten bde byed seri lung nang dang/hu'ai pyogs kyi gnas yig le'au gsum p'ao/

lam chen (rong) nang gi gnas bshad bstan (pa ni) md'a nas brag ser rtse mo dang leb steng ÷ mgon po bram giugs chen po vang byon yod ÷ de nas rong nang lag pa gyas p'ai phyogs ÷ (dzam) ser ne'au le dang bcas pa yod ÷ de 'ai mdun du dzam ser lha shug yod ÷ rong nang lha dbang brgya spyin sngas rgyas la ÷ phyul bas dung dkar gyas 'akhyil rang byon yod ÷ de nas yar la brag rong shin tu dog ÷ (hu'ai) sgra ni h'aum(phat) ngar sgra can ÷ gnas chen tsa (ri) rong gi chags tshul yin ÷ phan tshul ri gnyis zhing skyong yab yum gnas ÷ ri nag/

ngos la dmyal khams rang byon yod ÷ de nes yar la ston p'ai mdzad bcu yod ÷ md'a nas sgrol ma nyi shu rtsa gcig yod ÷ rang byon no mtshar che ba dpag med yod ÷ las ldan rnams la rang byon gang bsam mjal ÷ gnas rong gi le'au bzhi p'ao/

sa ma ya ÷ rgya O rgya O rgya ÷ bdag 'abri gung sngags 'chang rig pa 'aijan pa rtogs ldan chen mchog 'adus pa rtsal la ao rgyan thugs rje byin rlabs la rten nas/

rmi lam lung bstan byung nas chu mo bya lo zla tshes bzang por rnyed pa lags song/

sdeg can kur gyi rgyud pa phan par shog/

ai thi ÷ gzi yi bkris kun gzhi rnyog pa lvangs/

lam gyi bkra shis sku thig tshom bur shar/

'bras bu bkris lhun grub 'adus ma byas/

gdod m'ai rang zhal mijal b'ai bkris shog gnas yig 'adi 'abri gung chos rje so gsum pa rtogs ldan dkon mchog mchog thub bstan bstan p'ai rgyal mtsan la dag snang rmi lam gyi snang tshul bris pa 'adi rang tang 'adra b'ai gang zag rnams la phan phyir bris yin/

mkhas pa rnams kyi spyan lam du bzod par grol/

lung bstan 'adi yi tshig sogs la khri nan mi mdzang pa zhus/

sngon gyi gnas yig snying pa ri mkhas pa rnams kyi phyag la 'abyor na mdzad par zhus/

khrig nad can la dung ser por thong ba lta bu'ai gnas yig 'adi la dvgas rtogs ldan rin po che nas spyar p'ao/

Text in Roman Transliteration

Phu khar jong gi nas shad dag nang chu ze od gar zhes cha va zhugs so/

oh ah Hum Bajra (Vajra) Guru De Va Ta Ki Ni Na Mo Na Ma/

Ae Ma Ho/

zhi thog dang po chos ku kun du zang/

yod min tos dal lo das jod du med/

khor das nyis med sang lang re dog dal/

nang stong yer med kun zang yab yum stod/

aa las pad kar za dan hung yig las/

la ma dorje semppa gang ris ku/

te la nyi shar phog tar od zer gyi/

dig zang longs ku dorje sems pa stod/

nal gyi ma gos padme kyil nas thung/

gya bod lha srin tul ve thustob can/

pod dang Ladakh do va tham cat gyi cug nor pad jung tul pe ku la stod./

sngon tshe rig zin nus dan dorje chang/

mong de shegs mos pa tha yas zhabs/

dalta pa jung gyal shabs dog ban ngos/

jig dal ye shes dorje chor chod/

chogs su tu sum gyalva sras cas kyi/

thug je ye shes cig tu dus be gon dag gi drin cen tsa ya lama names/

mi del cyi vo sug gi gyan tu zhug/

de yan chad kyi chod jod kyi me tog song nas/

da nas shad ched pa poi gyu tsan kod pa ni/

Om Ah Huṃ Hum ÷ nag bar dang nyang pan ting zin zang/

tul pe ku chog ja tson ying po yis/

kye thing yin lom pad thing ta gyud pa/

nas yig kod pe choje togdan ngas/ ma aong loman rang dang kal nyam la/

phan pe lo yi ladakh shyam chogs nang phukhar Urgyan zong gi dub nas kyi/sngon gyi nas yig yod zhes gan rab kyis/shad kyang ladakh chinang sa tsans lang/

sngon dus ladakhas chosgyal gong ma nams/

balti pon dang phan tsun nang thugs yong/

ced nas nas dang tug lag khang la sogs/

thor kyen jung va nga rab nams kyis shad/

de chir nas shad gang yang mi dug go/

dad dan do nams nas jal chod bul la/

phebs mi nams la nas di do gyus dang/

rang jon nams kyang chen par dod na yang/

nas shad med pe dad mos ced nas log/chu dun leb kyang kom sel ma jed par/tong log do va je zhin nying je/

sam nas ma aong nas jal nams kyi don/nas shad rin chen theng va dag gis pel/nas shad dag nang di taro/

cung ba sum dan chu mo ca lo/

bod rab cung cu dun pa/

rab lo 966 chi lo 1993 bod da zhi pe shes nyi shu che da tug pe ches yin phu khar yul gyi yul chi nas urgyan jong gi dub de so mi rab nas la ngos shad zhu ve dus nas nang urgyan shogs khang chen poi nang sig dun sol debs dangs sog dang bjra gu ru thi char 30,000 cas gu ru rin po che la sol be bebs zhin nyi me chu shod nyis nas tsan gyi chu shod cu dang ched par tu chag chod dang del ve rang nyid cig bu thung la dad pa yin/

bod tses nyi shu cig nyin di dug la ma ge dun cu thag dang tshu ma cas dub de shog khang nang shogs khor gya chod sogs phul nas ta shis rab nas dang (thim) col sogs phul yin/

ngos rang dub phug te var thun la dod skabs rang gi sam pa la ngon lo tong thag ngon la sngayas nyis pa urgyan rin po che dir phebs nas cin labs zad pa skal pa zang kyang da ta nas di la nas shad sal po zhig cung na dad dan nams la phan pa dang sngayas kyi stan pa yang/

dar var nges sam zhing urgyan rin po che la sol ba deb zhin nas/

bav skabs zig la nyid la song va ta bu zhig jung rang la mi lam zhig thong ngos rang ngogs chang dorje zin pe cha lugs ched nas chag gyas la ta ma ru dar na nga dan chag yon na nang srid sal ve me long zhig rin po che du mi gyan dang dan pa dar kar ring va dang cas pa thog nas/

lho nub chogs kyi thang chen ser po zhig la do skabs/

thang kyil du chu mig dang sal yid du aong va zhig gi sar leb/

der nga rang ngal nas khas kom nas chu zhig tung ngo sam nas thung zhin pe skabs dun du kha do ma dar kar lha lhub gyon pa zhig chag yas na nor zong dang yon nas shel kar gyi thing va snams pa zhig jung/

bu nga ngo shes sam zhes sungs/

rang nyid nas sems ha cang ga va zhig la nas skabs gang yang zhu ma thub/de ma thag ngos kyi sems la nga skye va sngon dus kong pe yul du ter ton ja tshon snying poi skye va gyur skabs kyi ma dei dorje yudon me tul pa yin pa de rang gi ma yin par ngo shes/ngos kyi aa ma la red zhus yin/

ao derang yin/

da mi lo mang po das pe jes su ladags chi nang sa tshamgs su Urgyan gyi nas pu rig phugmo che nas dir bu rang dang thad pa nga re skyid/

sungs/

nor zhong de nga la nang/

da khyed rang gi dod pa tar nas de shad pa ngas ced chog/

dan pa ma jed pa yin la zung shig/

sungs nas gyes zum dangs dang cas nga la zig/ngos rang yang ma bu thad pa tar ga va jung na tamru gyan dan ma la phul yin/

ma nas bu rang gi me long legs pa de nang tos sungs nas/

ngai me long nang tas nas dad skabs/

Urgyan zong gi nas ri tham cad tha lham gyi shar/

lo gyus kyi da yig yang sal/

ao da bu rang gi me long nang ji ta va zhin zugs nyan dag ris dang dub phug gi chags tshul yibas sogs leng par dis/

maong dad dan nams la shod/

da nga rang lho nub zang tog pal ri urgyan rin po che dung du doao sung nas ngos kyi go la chag yas pe shad nas jes su ma bu nyis jal aong sung mi nang var gyur ro/

da me long nang gi nas shad kod pa ni/Ae Ma Ho ÷ Urgyan ma takki dag zong di ÷ ngon dus sangyas nyis pa padma jung ÷ Urgyan yul dang asha du ling yul ÷ zang ling kha che yul sogs cin labs skabs ÷ lo ni cig tong gu gya cig gi dus ÷ kha che yul gyi gyal po gho bi na ÷ lus la lu yi nad kyi zung ve dus ngags dang sman sogs gang yang ma phan nas ÷ urgyan yul nas padma jung nas zhus ÷ de tus ta din yang sang kyil khor sham ÷ gyal por vang nad sa dag don las dol ÷ pad jung je la gyal po ras dad na ÷ a sha du sha yul dang gil di yul ÷ chod pe nas su phul nas pad jung dang ÷ gyal po gho bi na cas nas dir phebs ÷ urgyang zong la purig phug mo zar ÷ lu dud ha la nag po nas sa yin ÷ kha che gyal la lu di nod pa na ÷ urgyan dir phab dam la tags pa yin ÷ ta chag khyung ling zhes pe dag ri di ÷ dub phu chen poi yon la yod pa yin ÷ dag gi leb la shin je chos gyal gyi ÷ me long jal dan bur la jal va yod ÷ dei steng thovo+din sal va yod ÷ ta din yas la gya gar pan chen ni ÷ pi ma mi tai ku zugs yon zigs yod ÷ dei aog nas ta phag zhal jor yod ÷ dei aog na kha do seng dong yod ÷ dei aog la jo yu don la ÷ tsho mo che la chag na da dar nam ÷ yon la kha do chung va nyis zhugs yod ÷ dog ri zhung la ka gyad de dus sku ÷ sal bar zhugs yod dei dun ngos na ÷ je tsun mi la gom thag rang dig zhugs ÷ dei sten na gyal va god cang zhugs ÷ de nas yas kyi dag nag mar poi bar ÷ drigung skyo ba jig sten gon po zhug ÷ dei steng na do rje chang chen yot ÷ ka gyad yod gyi tha me dag leb na ÷ ka gyud yongs kyi stan srung lha mo yot ÷ dei tse la shug pe vu dugs yod ÷ dei steng na dag zur ngo jam la ÷ padma kar poi sku nyan sal va yod ÷ ri tsa var sangyas stan pa yis ÷ cin dag ha shang ha thug skar va yod ÷ shin je chosgyal me long yon chogs na ÷ dus sum sangyas sku nyan sal bar yod ÷ dei aog ma nas srug ma mo dam can dang ÷ za chen khyab jug bu gu dan pa yod ÷ de nas lung pai pho dang bu tse la ÷ zeg pai lam na lu dud cho thul gyi ÷ dul gyi zung nyan rin thung dungyad yod de na yar la song nas ta din phug ÷ chag dor phug zhes phug pa nyis del yod ÷ dei nang don zhi ve zang dug sman ÷ dog zhin sa ngags cin labs dan pa yod ÷ sa ngags nang nas urgyan rinpoche ÷ bu ta kar po khando ma tshogyal gyi ÷ bu ta nag po yin labs skabs rin thob ÷ phug nyis yas na ca khyung ga ru ta ÷ sku yi zugs nyan dag la thim pa yod ÷ de nams lu dud tul ve tags ni yin ÷ kha che yu gyi gyal po gho bi ni ÷ nad las dol ve lo gyus zhin du ni ÷ rang jon nams ta chag ling la zigs ÷ togs dan chog tul ngags chang kon chog thub stan pe gyal tsan gyi nas shad sar du che ve leu dang po ao ÷ ta chag ling gi bu tse re de ni ÷ yi dam sang va dus pe pho dang yin ÷ dei dun na shar gyi kar khung zhes ÷ dag la ukhang yod pa ngo tshar zhugs ÷ pho dang te va do je keu chang di ÷ chags tshul rim ba cung zhig dar shad na ÷ pho dang tshan la ma ra takki dzang ÷ yibs ni chi tar sittai yibs su yong ÷ sittai yibs aog pho dang la gam jugs ÷ vang gi kyil khor thab dang dra va yod ÷ dei jur sam pho dang te va yi ÷ dag phug sten aog nyis dan cin labs can ÷ urgyan da dun zhag dun ting zin zhugs ÷ kha doe am yig me long nang na sal ÷ dag phug nang ni mi yi cang khog zhin ÷ ci vo de chen khor loe tsa dabs yod ÷ din pa lonscod khor loe tsa dabs yod ÷ nying kha chos kyi khor loe tsa dabs yod ÷ snying gi thod du gu rui tshe bum gyi ÷ rang jon shin tu sal va jal gyu yod ÷ urgyan rin po che yi tshe dub ni ÷ yang sang nyi da gaui tshe dub dzad ÷ pad gyal chi nang sang ve dub khog dang ÷ cang sems kar mar ter jas khyad phags sogs ÷ ————————

ter nams yod pa me long nang nas sal ÷ ter dag lu dud doje du don dang ÷ ka sung sum gyi ca ra ced zhin yod ÷ phur gyud pu ti yang sang dus pa dang ÷ du phur dzas rig phung kun dol gyi ÷ dam dzas khyad phags nas nang zhugs pa yod ÷ ma aong ter gyur ston——————zhes ca jung gyur na ÷ ten del zom zhing par chad med na phebs ÷ ai de aog te va tul pa khor lo yod ÷ la yas la yon rus yibs bu kha nyis ÷ phan tshun doe dag phug di nyis yin ÷ sang nas de skyong khor loe yibs go nas ÷ chi la thon pae dag phug gya go yin ÷ gyab kyi tsa khung phug bae yas tag nas ÷ tog dan ngos kyi chag jes som yod ÷ do nams pal rir urgyan chen poe drung ÷ jal ve ten del dig pe mon lam yin ÷ sang ngags ma zas mang du jung va de ÷ do va su yi cod kyang ngan song med ÷ dub chu che med dud tsi gyun bas di ÷ tshes cu dus chod nams la mang var jung ÷ bu tser shug pa dugs kyi yibs can yod ÷ dei stong na stan sung cag men yod ÷ pho dang te va da phug ma ra tkki zong gi nas shad leu nyis pao ÷ pho dang nas kyi te ve yas chogs na ÷ ta din chag dor ling gi aog gi dag ÷ bus na tsho gyal phug pa zhes ca yod ÷ dei nang urgyan padme sku jes yod ÷ de nas yon la jam yang ral di yod ÷ sku jes dun na kha doae tshogs khor yod ÷ tshogs chang dut tsi bar med bas pa yod ÷ de nas yas do mar babs lam kha na ÷ cang chub chod ten rang jon sal ba yod ÷ chod ten te steng do va su do na ÷ tse di dig cang shi na ngan song med ÷ rig dug nas den ced dang da bao ÷ dei yas na las das kar nag gi ÷ ge teg kar nag tags pai khung nyis ÷ cig nas zul nas cig nas thon sa yod ÷ mi dogs med par thar na las dag yin ÷ par la tsir ve pi pi dorje yod ÷ de yis tsir na dig pa shags la bad ÷ de la ma thog la ni yang va yin ÷ deng sang me nams gyi drang po log pa zer/

ga va gom nas ge la tson par ja ÷ cang chub sems dang ma dal tan por zung dei aog na ting zin phug pa yod ÷ jam jangs dub na shis rab myur du phel ÷ dei sten yar la thon po dag kyib na ÷ yar ngo mar ngoi tshes dangs tags pe chir ÷ 卐 yung drung shal la bris dan pa shar zhin yod ÷ yar ngo tshas cig nas ni co nge bar ÷ 卐 yung drung dun shar shin tu sal va yod ÷ mar ngo cu drug nas ni nam gang bar ÷ rim gyi rim gyi med par gyur ba yin ÷ yees cho gyal dag phug aog nas ÷ drag nag leb al zhi dag jo mo ni ÷

spun sun zugs kyi ri mo rang jon yod ÷ de nas yi ge Om Aa Hum sum yod ÷ lar yang Om Aa Hum sum ni ÷ tse nas yod pe rang jon ngo tshar yod ÷ gu rus jin labs zad pa du sum yin ÷ kha che chos gyal gho bi na la ni ÷ vang zhi gyur cir sku sum ngo tod nas ÷ urgyan la lob ta va cen med gyur dongs long yed med gyur pe du sum yin ÷ kha che chos gyal gho be na yi dus ÷ yi ge rang jon da yig sal po yod ÷ ————yi ge zugs ni del tar jal gyu yod ÷ gyal po di yi nga aog gyal stan dar ÷ nas di yan lag kha pal kar jo ang yod ÷ dei yas na bjara gu ru dang ÷ yig drug rang jon shin tu sal pa yod ÷ de aog stong chen poi nye dabs na ÷ gu ru chag jes zhabs jes sal ba yon ÷ nas la do ve lam gyi yas chogs na ÷ dag dog dang ser ngo jam leb la ni ka dam chod ten bang rim can zig yod ÷ cung zhig aog nas shug dong chen po yod ÷ de ni chosgyal sku ngai lha shug yin ÷ dei dun na thu mig yan lag gyad ÷ thang bas tig cang lhai dud tshi yod ÷ de nas yar la lung pe nang song nas gon khang phug zer carog rang yod ÷ stan srung ma ha kaliyi dub nas yin ÷ dei sting gi ri bo tshog zhing yibs ÷ ka gyud la ma dorje chang chen nas ÷ te lo na ro mar mi dags po sogs ÷ zhugs pa ka gyud pho dang zhes su dags dei yas na dag ni gon pe yibs ÷ ling gi ga sar gyal poi pho dang yin ÷ dun na mi chen lags drai dag cig yod ÷ de ni ling gi pao bo dan ma yin ÷ deng sang hal gyi la ni zer va mul bhi rong la do sa na yod/da yas nas stan cu dug dag ri yod ÷ de nas de chog khor loi pho dang yod ÷ dei yas na cang sems chen po/

gyad ÷ zugs pe dag ri ngo tshar che va yod ÷ de'aog dag ri kun ga re ve nang ÷ can ras zigs sku chag tong cang tong yod ÷ dei nas zur dag kar ngo jam la ÷ stan srung Aa chi me long snam pa yod ÷ de nas dag ri tshogs kyi yibs ta bur ÷ ngo la chod me rang jon khyad par yod ÷ dub de gon nas tshan la jal na kun gyi sal po jal zhing de mo thong ÷ (sa ri tse phu) lung chen phu mi can ras zigs vang gi ÷ pho dang po ta la zhes tshan tu sol ÷ sngon dus gyal va god tshang lob ma chog ÷ dub thob chen po urgyan pa zhes pa ÷ urgyan kha che yul nas der phebs nas ÷ sa ri lung nang thams khang cin dan nang ÷ da va sum dang ched kha lhag sam zhugs ÷ dub chen urgyan ter nas zhes pe sku ÷ rang jon ka ma ru pai can ras zigs ÷ chag zhi pa dei cin labs shin tu che ÷ do va su yi jal yang ngan song med ÷ sa chu do la me bar sogs kyang yod ÷ sa ri nang gi ÷ shamgs khang dang dub thob urgyan phebs dug da va sum lag zhugs pe lo gyus de me long nang gi dag nang dis pa yin/

lung chen nang gi chod ten bang rim can ÷ ri de gya gar chod ten de jed sari lung nang dang phui chog kyi nas yig leu sum pao/

lam chen rong nang gi nas shad stan pa ni da nas dag ser tse mo dang leb steng ÷ gon po dam jugs chen po rang jon yod ÷ de nas rong nang lag pa yas pa chogs ÷ zam ser neu le dang cas pa yod ÷ dei dun du zam ser lha shug yod ÷ rong nang lha vang gya cin sangyas la ÷ phul vas dung kar yas khyil rang jon yon ÷ de nas yar la dag rong shin tu dog ÷ chui da ni hum phat ngar da can ÷ nas chen tsa ri rong gi chags tshul yin ÷ phan tshun ri nyis zhing skyong yab yum nas ÷ ri nag/ngos la myal khams rang jon yod ÷ de nas yar la ston pe dzad cu yod ÷ da nas dol ma yi shu tsa cig yod rang jon no tshar che va pag med yod ÷ las dan nams la rang jon gang sam jal ÷ nas rong gi leu zhi pao/

sa ma ya ÷ gya gya gya dag dri gung ngags chang rig pa jin pa togs dan chen chog dus pa tsal la urgyan thugs je cin labs la ten nas/

mi lam lung stan jung nas chu mo ca lo za tshes zang por nyed pa lags song/

deg can kur gyi gyud pa phan par shog/

ai thi ÷ zi yi tis kun zhi nyog pa dangs/

lam gyi ta shis sku thig tshom bur shar/

das bu tis lhun dub dus ma cas/

dod me rang zhal jal ve ta sis shog nas yig di drigung chos je so sum pa tog dan kon chog thub stan stan pe gyal tsan la dag nang mi lam gyi nang tshul dis pa di rang tang da be gang zag nams la phan chir dis yin/

khas pa nams kyi can lam du zod par sol/

lung stang di yi tshig sogs la thi nan mi zag pa zhus/

ngon gyi nas yig nying pa re khas pa nams kyi chag la jor na zad par zhus/

thig nad can la dung ser por thong va ta bui nas yig di ladakh togdan rin po che nas char pao/

geo/

Translation

One night a devotee saw Lhamo (Devi) in his dream,she was saying:

"Son! Earlier you were Dorje Yudon, your name was Ster Ton Zha Chon Ningbo, was born at the border of Purang and Purig."

The border place is Phokarzong, lies at the above said border. A Buddhist monastery is built here. Every year thousands devotees visited to see the monastery and Syambhu Buddhist deities, engraved on the mountain rocks.

On April 1993 for the welfare of devotees Phokarzong village committee decided to print the details about the above Buddhist deities and the concerned spiritual places. Here follows the brief translation of the above manuscript.

Om Aa Hum Vajra Guru Deva Takini Namo Namah.

Ae Ma Hum.

Salute to Zhi Thog; chos ku kun du zang yod min tos dal lo das jod du med, kor das nyis med sang lang re dog dal, nang stong yer med kun zang yab yum stod, aa las pad ka za dan hung yig las and lama Dorje Sempa.

Rig zin lama Dorje Sempa was born on lotus. He was a great saint, his engraved white figure on mountain rock shines more brightly in presence of sun. The great siddha will safe human beings from all evil spirits. In Ladakh and Tibet people consider him as second Buddha. Villagers of Phokarzong pray to bless them in all occasions.

People belief Padmasambhava was a great yogi, he preached his followers time and again. One thousand years ago he visited Phokarzong and went for meditation. Buddhists have strong faith upon him and offer prayer on every auspicious occasions.

In one occasion vajra guru along with lamas and chomos (Nuns) chanted 30,000 mantra beads. Besides, Guru rinpoche offered morning prayer and chanted mantra beats till late night.

Once Dorje Chang came in the dream of a devotee.He had *damaru* in his left hand and *dadar* in right, weared valuable clothes, seemed as if he was going to the south-west of the Phokarzong. Soonafter, arrived at a big plain, near the lake. He was thirsty, to quench his thirst as he sat and put his hand into the lake, Khandoma (goddess) appeared. She had weared beautiful clothes, held milk pot in her right hand and a bead in her left, said:

"I know Phokarzong is the place where Buddhist and Muslim country border touch each other."

To acknowledge the dream Dorje chang thought:

"In his previous birth he was born as Yudon in Kongpo village, was later popularly known Khandoma."

Buddhists have faith that about 1300 years ago king Ghobina kingdom was located at the east of Purig. Once king decided to visit Asha Doling village. On his way he forgot to bow his head before Nagraj. As a result Nagraj became angree and cursed him. King's legs paralysed and could not walk further. Thus, was taken back to his palace, doctors treated him, when king's health was not improved his advisers suggested him to call Padmasambhava. Accordingly king sent his one minister to Urgyana. After meeting with Padmasambhava, he requested:

"Guruji Pranam, my king Ghobina is suffering with the serious leg pain, his legs are perfectly paralysed, and can't move. Therefore, kindly bless him."

Padmasambhava listened him peacefully, and replyed:

"I understand king's problem. I'll go there".

Padmasambhava arrived Purig with Ghobina's minister. After meeting with king Ghobina he performed Kalacakra *puja*. Gradually king Ghobina felt some improvement, soonafter he started walking. He was very much pleased with Padmasambhava.Later gave Asha Thusa and Gildi areas in gift.

Black Nagaraja who lived in the king Ghobina kingdom, disturbed the freedom of his citizens. Consequently every year many of them suffered by several diseases. Padmasambhava stopped his activities and declared the whole region free from Nagas and renamed the kingdom as 'Purig Phamo'.

In Purig Phamo, nearby to Phokarzong has stag-tsang khyungling mountain. The following Buddhist deities are engraved on this mountains.

1. Yamantaka and Standin (main figures)
2. Gegar Panchen] on the right of center
3. Bima Miti] Figures
4. Khandoma- On the left of center figures.
5. Staphak – Holds bow and arrow] Below the
6. Como cho - Holds bow and arrow] above figures

Besides, the following carvings can be seen

(i) Eight forms of Padmasambhava

(ii) Melarepa (Meditation mudra)

(iii) Geva Gocangpa (Siddha)

(iv) Skyova Digsten Gonpa (Head of Drigungpa)

(v) Dorje chang

(vi) Stag-tshang

A room is also made of peacock feathers and wooden beams at the corner of the above mountain. Here following images are engraved.

(i) Hasang

(ii) Hatuk

(iii) Padma karpo

(iv) Khyabjung

(v) Yamantaka

(vi) Tusung Sangyas

(vii) Chosgyal

On the way to Phokarzong, there is a carving of Naga and two caves of chagdor on the rock just above the nala. It is said those who suffer from any disease if eat chogs (Prasad) of chagdor may get relief from the disease. Inside the caves one can finds Padmasambhava's white hair, Khandoma's black hair and cakung's two engraved figures.

Garuda is the enemy of Naga, his presence stop the activities of Nagas in the region. The details of king Ghobina description that how Padmasambhava cured him can be seen in the above said caves.

Yamantaka palace is carved on the mid of stag-tsang ling mountain. The said palace is facing to the east. The engraved holes represent windows.

The Phokarzang is also known as 'Marathaki Jor'. It looks like human back. Its kitchen represents kalcakra, top and bottom of this cave are popular pilgrim centers.

Padmasambhava meditated for seven days in Phokarzong. This cave is expressed in the following way:

1. Dechok Khorlo stap chat –the middles portion or the stomatch of cave.

2. Long chot khorla – Near the top or at the neck of the cave.

3. Choskyi khordo-Near the middle or at the naval of the cave.

4. Padmasambhava's pot : Near the middle or near the naval of the cave.

5. 'Om' shaped mirror : The said cave looks 'Om' mantra shaped from distance.

All the above spiritual things are naturally made, therefore worshipped by the devotees.

Phokarzang is important because Padmasambhava with his spiritual power tied Nagaraj by rope through his nose. Later the two following images carved here:

(i) Dorje Yudon : Holds Khorlo

(ii) Dorje : At the upper side of Yudon

Phokarzong is a center of various Buddhist deities or rather to say it has treasury of ritual things. The village is situated at the base of the above mountain.

Devotees have faith that by visiting Phokarzong their future life become bright and no enemy can harm them. There are many Buddhist tantric mandalas in which siddhas meditated in the two caves. Here follows the details :

The two caves of Phokarzong are made in such a way that devotee can enter by one cave but can't return from the same, therefore, he/she has to come out from the other cave. These caves look like a woman uterus from distance.

If a devotee follow the above caves, may acknowledge that they join at one place, then turns into a big one.

Devotees believe that in the said cave Buddha in the form of Dorje chang gave Tantric preaching. Therefore many yogis retreated here, some of them got place in Padmasambhava mandala. Besides, there is Togdan dogi's pot and sacret spring water which flows throughout the year. The volume of the water increases during 8,10,15 and 30th day of the 10th month of the year of Tibetan calendar. One finds *shukpa* tree at the water source, it helps to protect it from dryness. In fact devotees express the Phokarzong cave as king of sea. It has three portions which represent three Buddhist deities/gurus.

1. Middle portion – Heygriva
2. Right portion- Padmasambhava
3. Left portion – Vajrapani

Phokarzong is a pious cave in Purig. Padmasambhava meditated here. By virtue of this here we can see his body impression. We can devide the cave according to its spritual importance into three portions:

1. Middle portion : Wine filtered in olden days.
2. Righ portion : Manjusri impression.
3. Left portion : Khando chokhor.

The cave has Syambhu Changcub Chorten, whoever pass through this chorten may rid from sin and never takes birth in Hell, Idak and Animal Lokas.

The center part of the cave is narrow like woman's breast and is known vajra. Devotee who pass through this difficult way may gets relief from sufferings as Angulimal got relief from all immoral acts after the blessing of Buddha. One, if goes further inside the cave may see two more caves belong to 'sin' and 'Puniya'. Devotee who meditate Manjusri here may gets Buddhicitta.

According to Tibetan Calendar during yarnas (one to fifteen) Savastika's appear on the Phokarzang. Seven of them look bright in presence of sun light. During Mar-ngos (i.e. 15 to 30) their size decrease day by day, finally on Namkhang disappear.

Behind the Phokarzong, there is a natural lake and below this a black, hard rock. Besides, three Om Aa Hum mantras are engraved on the Phokarzong cave by the blessing of Padmasambhava. They are :

(i) At the top center of the cave.

(ii) Lower portion of the cave.

(iii) Lower portion of the cave.

Buddhist pilgrims have the following point of opinion that- "By the blessing and rituals of Padmasambhava when king Ghobina's health improved, he later became his disciple. Then Padmasambhava gave him teachings on 'Lung gyi' tenba and Tog pe tenba'."

In addition we can see the following religions carvings on the left and right of 'kha pal kar jong' in the said cave:

1.	Vajra guru Padmasambhava	Right of 'kha pal kar jong'
2.	Mani Padma	

3. Kadam chorten : Engraved on yellow stone at the left of 'kha pal kar jong'.

4. Hands print of Padmasambhava and shukpa tree : At the right of 'kha pal kar jon 'and just below the vajra guru Padmasambhava.

The shukpa tree is important because it was the home of Dharmaraj Lhashuk. By virtue of this 'nya la gyaldan' spring water comes into the cave. This water is as pure as Heaven's water. Further inside the cave we can see the carvings of 'carok rangcon gonpa' and Mahakali. On the nearby mountain the following carvings can be seen:

1. Tathagata throne : On the mountain top
2. Dorje
3. Tilo
4. Naro
5. Marpa
6. Mila

(Items 2–6) Just below the above throne.

7. Lha-khang and Gelam Kesar's palace ; On the mountain left of Phokarzong.
8. Kesar's heros : They are carved nearby Kesar's palace

There are some more carvings on both side rocks of the Phokarzong on way to Mulbek. The details is cited below:

1. 16 Arhats
2. Dechok Khorlo Demba's palace: on the left of Arhats
3. Eight Bodhisattvas : On the right of the Arhats
4. Thousand eyes and hands Avalokitesvara : Below the above carved images
5. Achi choskyi Dolma : seated with mirror carved on soft mountain rock
6. Lighted lamp and chog (Prasad) : They are carved before the above deities.

Any devotee if follows the above path may reach near the Avalokitesvara's palace.

Buddhist pilgrims have faith that once Dharmaraj Gochang's disciple visited the above cave. He came here from Urgyan *Desa* (country.) His chamkhang still can be seen. Thereafter, another siddha meditated here for three and half months. He brought Padmasambhava statue.

The four hands Avalokitesvara statue of this cave is famous among devotees, they say:

"Those who able to see the above statue, get *puniya* and rid from the Bhava cakra."

It is said during king Ashoka period, his one messenger built a chorten in Phokarzong subsequently many syambhu images engraved. Here follows the details:

1. Gonpo Damjug Chenmo
2. Zambala — Right to the mountain
3. Goddess
4. Zambala lakshuk — nearby to the above mountain.
5. Nawang Gyabjin
6. Buddha's Umbrella
7. Sing-du

In a nut shell Phokarzong is a pious place, has a ability to generate fire after the collision of water, earth and air. The pass on the mountain is known 'Nechen cari Rong' in which 'Zim khyong yab-yum' lived. Besides, ' Hum Phet' mantra is carved alongwith various Buddhist deities and gurus.

Bibliography

Francke, A.H. 'History of Western Tibet', London, 1907.

Jina, Prem Singh: 'Ladakh Aur Paryatan' (Tourism in Ladakh), In 1st National Conferences, CIBS, Leh-Ladakh, 1981.

Jina, Prem Singh : 'Ladakh Sanskriti per Seemant Sanskriti ka Prabhav', News Letters, New Delhi, Sept-Oct, 1982.

Jina, Prem Singh : 'Bhagwan Buddha kaha,' Dinman, Times of India Pub., New Delhi, 28th Nov-4th December, 1982.

Jina, Prem Singh: 'Santi Stupa Ladakh ke', Yojana, Jammu, March, 1983.

Jina, Prem Singh : Boudh Bikshu of Ladakh', In All India Conference, Delhi Univ., Delhi, 1983.

Jina, Prem Singh : 'Seet kal me Leh Ghati', Sheeraja-65, Jammu, March, 1983.

Jina, Prem Singh: 'The Foreign Tourist Traffic in Ladakh', Himalayan Reseach and Development (Problem Oriented Studies), Vol. 3(i), Nainital, June, 1984.

Jina, Prem Singh : 'Buddhism in Ladakh and World Peace', in 10th International Buddhist Conference on Buddhism and World Peace, Japanese Temple, Bodh Gaya, Vol. X, 1984.

Jina, Prem Singh : 'Astangik Mary aur Moksa', Prakashitman, Delhi, March, 1984.

Jina, Prem Singh : 'Foreign Tourists and their Impact on Ladakh', in IIIrd National Conference Proceed. Ladakh Prabha (3), 1985.

Jina, Prem Singh : 'A Brief Introduction of Ladakh Gonpas', In: 'Ladakh: Life and Culture,; K.N. Pandit (ed.), Kashmir University, Srinagar: 39-50.

Jina, Prem Singh: 'Economic and Cultural Relations between Ladakh and Lahul and Spiti,; In: Ist All India Conference at Baudh Darshan Mahavidayalaya, Keylong (H.P.).

Jina, Prem Singh: 'A Survey of Buddhist Community in Ladakh Himalaya', In: 12th International Buddhist Conference on Buddhism and Social Harmony, Japanese Temple, Bodh Gaya, India, Vol. XII, 1986.

Jina, Prem Singh: 'Pasturelands of Zangskar and its effects on Ecology,; In : Ist National Conference, Leh-Ladakh, 1986.

Jina, Prem Singh and Mir, A.A.: Pasturelands of Leh and its effects of Ecology in Ist National Conference by Indian Army, Trishul Nature Conservation, Leh-Ladakh, 1986.

Jina, Prem Singh: 'Monasteries in the Economy of Leh-Ladakh; In: All India conference on 'Buddhist Monasteries of Himalayan Region: Various Aspect,; 9-13th August, CIBS, Leh, 1988.

Jina, Prem Singh : 'Bodh Dham Leh-Ladakh', Hindu Chetna, Vol.7, New Delhi, Jina, 1988: 21-33.

Jina, Prem Singh : 'Ladakhi Rajao ka Bodh Dham me yogdan', Hindu Chetna, Vol. 10, Sept. 1988:19-20.

Jina, Prem Singh : 'Eco-environmental study of Tourist Industry in Ladakh Himalaya', In: All India Conference, Kashmir University, Srinagar, Deptt. of Centre for Central Asian Studies, 1989.

Jina, Prem Singh: 'Pasture Ecology of Leh-Ladakh', In Wessenschalts Gegschiche and Gegenwarlige Forschungen in Nordwest Indian Saatliches Museum for Volkerkunde, Dresden Forshungstelle, Germany, 1990.

Jina, Prem Singh : 'Ladakh me Bodh Kala Ka Udbhav aur Vikash'; Sheeraja, Feb-March, Vol. 1991: 12-14.

Jina, Prem Singh: 'History and Growth of Education', Himalaya Today, Nov. 1991:16-18.

Jina, Prem Singh : 'Ladakh ki Mahila Prashashak Putith Wang mo', Hamara Sahitya' Jammu, 1992:104-06.

Jina, Prem Singh : 'Impact of Tourism on Ladakh Society and Culture'; In: All India Conference, JNU, New Delhi, 1993.

Jina, Prem Singh: 'Poultry Industry in Ladakh Himalaya'; Himalaya Today, Sept. 92. Feb.1993, Vol.IX, No. 2 and 3, 1993: 7.

Jina, Prem Singh: 'Dasvi Satabdi Purva Lahul me Bodh Dharm evam Sanskriti; Janjati Mela Smarika; 1993: 60-62.

Jina, Prem Singh: 'Tourism in Ladakh Himalaya'; Indus Publishing Company, New Delhi, 1994.

Jina, Prem Singh and Konchok Namgyal: 'Spiti ka Sanskritik Itihas', Janyati Utsav, 1994:70-72.

Jina, Prem Singh : 'Buddhism in Ladakh and its Approach to the Material world' In ; 'Buddhism Approach to the Material World', proceed of the 18th International Buddhist Conference, Vol. XVIII; Bodh Gaya, 1993-94:51-60.

Jina, Prem Singh: 'Bhiksuni Sangha Avam Ladakh me Usaki Stithi',; Proceed, of the National Conference, 1994; 50-52.

Jina, Prem Singh: 'Kesar Aek Mahakaviya', Sheeraja, Vol.II, June-July, Jammu, 1994.

Jina, Prem Singh: 'High Pasturelands of Ladakh Himalaya'; Indus Pub.Co.New Delhi; 1995.

Jina, Prem Singh and Konchok Namgyal : Phyang Monastery of Ladakh; Indus Pub.Co. New Delhi, 1995.

Jina, Prem Singh : 'Buddhism in Ladakh'; Yug Udbodhan, Vol.I., No.9, New Delhi, 1995:14-16.

Jina, Prem Singh: 'Ladakh: The Land and the People'; Indus Pub.Co. New Delhi, 1996.

Jina, Prem Singh: 'Hemis: The Biggest Buddhist Monastery of Ladakh',Yug Udbodhan, Vol. 2, No. 4., New Delhi, 1996:15.

Jina, Prem Singh : 'Ladakh Gonpao me Bikhsunio ki Pravesh Vidhi', Yug Udbodhan, Vol.2, No.6, New Delhi, 1996: 9.

Jina, Prem Singh: 'Taho Monastery-A Unique Monument in Spiti Valley', Yug Udbodhan, Vol. 2, No.11, New Delhi, 1996:13.

Jina, Prem Singh (ed.) : 'Recent Researchers on the Himalaya'; Indus Pub.Co., New Delhi; 1997.

Jina, Prem Singh : 'Tibetan Manuscripts and Inscriptions on Ladakh Himalaya', Sri Satguru Pub., New Delhi, 1998.

Jina, Prem Singh; 'Some Monasteries of Drigung pa order in Central Ladakh', Sri Satguru Pub., New Delhi, 1999.

Jina, Prem Singh: 'Changing Face of Ladakh Himalaya', Om Pub., New Delhi, 1999.

Jina, Prem Singh and Konchok Namgyal: 'Lamaguru Monastery of Ladakh Himalaya', Om Pub., New Delhi, 1999.

Jina, Prem Singh: 'Ladakh Mera Anubhav', (My Experience in Ladakh), Anjuri, 1999.

Jina, Prem Singh: 'History of Education and Growth in Ladakh', International Conference, IALS, Leh-Ladakh, 1999.

Jina, Prem Singh : 'Ladakh : Past and Present', Gyan Pub., New Delhi, 2000.

Jina, Prem Singh: 'Varsha vas ka Mahatava', All India Conference on 'Trisavana', CIBS, Leh-Ladakh, 2001.

Jina, Prem Singh : 'Buddhism and Science, National Seminar on Role and Contribution of Buddhism and Vedic Dharma in National Integration; Ladakh Phandey Tsogspa, 2001.

Jina, Prem Singh : 'Tibetan Inscriptions in Diskit Monastery, Nubra (Ladakh) 63rd Indian History Congress, 2002.

Jina, Prem Singh : 'Religious History of Ladakh Himalaya', Sri Satguru Pub., New Delhi, 2001.

Jina, Prem Singh: 'Development of Ladakh: Recent Reseachers', Kalpaz Pub., New Delhi, 2002.

Jina, Prem Singh: 'First Hand Tibetan Inscriptions on Rock & Stones of Ladakh Himalaya', Sri Satguru Pub., New Delhi, 2003.

Jina, Prem Singh: 'Tibetan Inscriptions in Chomoling Temple of Thiksey monastery of Ladakh Himalaya', 64th Indian History Congress.

Jina, Prem Singh : 'Buddhism and Female Education', XXVIII. International Buddhist Conference, Indosan Nipponji, Bodh Gaya, 2003.

Jina, Prem Singh: 'History of Education before 1947 in Ladakh', National Conference, CIBS, 2002.

Jina, Prem Singh: 'Kesar : Atihasik Upaniyas', Sakshi Prakashan, Delhi, 2004.

Jina, Prem Singh: 'Buddhism in the Twenty First century', 'International Conference, CIBS, 2004.

Jina, Prem Singh : 'Chomoling temple ka Adhiyan; In : All India Conference, CIBS, 2005.

Jina, Prem Singh : 'Ladakh Profile', Kalpaz Pub., New Delhi, 2005.

Jina, Prem Singh: 'Buddhist Paintings in Gurpug monastery in Ladakh', In International Conference, Japanese Temple, 2005.

Jina, Prem Singh: 'Car Brahma Vihara', In : All India Conference, CIBS, Leh, 2006.

Jina, Prem Singh: 'Paintings in Nyingpa Lhakhang of Mangtrao Monastery of Ladakh, International Conference, Japanese Temple, 2006.

Jina, Prem Singh: 'Ladakh Himalaya: Past and Present', Anmol Pub., New Delhi, 2006.

Jina, Prem Singh : 'Tourist Resources of Ladakh', Anmol Pub., New Delhi, 2007.

Jina, Prem Singh : 'Thiksey monastery of Ladakh Himalaya', Sri Satguru Pub. New Delhi, 2007.

Jina, Prem Singh : 'Tourism and Buddhist monastries of Ladakh', Kalpaz Pub., New Delhi; 2007.

Jina, Prem Singh : 'Buddhism in Lahul', Sri Satguru Pub., New Delhi (in press).

Index